LONGMAN
English Works

WORKBOOK

2

Sally Burgess

Robert O'Neill

Longman

Contents

Review Unit (pp4–7)
Grammar: question words
Grammar: questions with *how*
Grammar: pronouns
Grammar: sentences with *going to*
Grammar: adverbs of frequency
Vocabulary: odd one out
Spelling
Vocabulary: words that go together
Conversation management: personal information
Grammar: questions
Writing: job application

Unit 1 (pp8–10)
Conversation management: an interview
Grammar: questions
Writing: personal information
Vocabulary: opposites
Spelling
Sounds and spelling
Grammar: sentences with *need* and *should*
Vocabulary: words that go together
Grammar: *as, than, of, from*

Unit 2 (pp11–13)
Conversation management: telephone language
Vocabulary: words that go together
Grammar: Present Progressive
Vocabulary: words that go together
Spelling
Vocabulary: opposites
Grammar: questions
Writing: fax messages

Unit 3 (pp14–16)
Conversation management: arrangements
Grammar: *would, could, Let's*
Grammar: *may*
Vocabulary: words that go together
Grammar: *used to*
Sounds and spelling
Writing: formal letter

Unit 4 (pp17–19)
Conversation management: typical responses
Grammar: verb forms
Grammar: Present Perfect/Past Simple
Grammar: questions and answers
Vocabulary: words that go together
Grammar: adjectives and adverbs
Writing: memo; prepositions

Test 1 (p20)
A Grammar
B Vocabulary
C Spelling and word formation
D Writing

Unit 5 (pp21–23)
Conversation management: at a hotel reception
Grammar: verb tenses
Work and leisure
Grammar: Present Perfect, Past Simple, *used to do*
Vocabulary: words that go together
Grammar: verbs and nouns
Writing: dates and addresses

Unit 6 (pp24–26)
Conversation management: problems and sympathy
Grammar: *I don't know . . .* + question word
Vocabulary: sentences with *feel*
Grammar: prepositions
Grammar: indirect questions
Vocabulary: *communicate, inform, notify, contact*
Spelling
Writing: verb forms; formal letters

Unit 7 (pp27–29)
Conversation management: a survey
Grammar: question word + *do you think . . . ?*
Vocabulary: expressions with *reason, cause, result, effect*
Grammar: first conditionals
Grammar: cause and effect
Vocabulary: *spend, waste, lose, give up*
Writing: formal letter

Unit 8 (pp30–32)
Conversation management: talking it over
Grammar: passive
Vocabulary: opposites
Spelling
Vocabulary: opposites
Grammar: questions and answers
Grammar: prepositions
Writing: completing a form

Contents

Test 2 (p33)
A Grammar
B Spelling and pronunciation
C Vocabulary
D Writing

Unit 9 (pp34–36)
Conversation management: doctor and patient
Grammar: Past Progressive
Grammar: Past Progressive and Past Simple
Vocabulary: *ache, pain, hurt, damage*
Sounds and spelling
Grammar: *each other/themselves*
Vocabulary: parts of the body
Writing: description of injury

Unit 10 (pp37–39)
Conversation management: telephone conversation
Vocabulary: request or demand?
Grammar: reported speech
Vocabulary: words that go together
Spelling
Grammar: second conditionals
Vocabulary: *steal, rob, thief, burglar, pickpocket, shoplifter*
Writing: memo

Unit 11 (pp40–42)
Conversation management: offers
Grammar: *Shall I . . . ?*
Vocabulary: *think, suppose, hope*
Sounds and spelling
Vocabulary: jobs
Grammar: adjectives and adverbs
Vocabulary: words that go together
Writing: job applications

Unit 12 (pp43–45)
Conversation management: an interview
Grammar: questions with *who* and *what*
Vocabulary: adjectives and nouns
Spelling
Grammar: Present Perfect Progressive with *for* and *since*
Vocabulary: numbers
Writing: expanding notes

Test 3 (p46)
A Grammar
B Vocabulary
C Spelling and word formation
D Writing

Unit 13 (pp47–49)
Conversation management: speaking to the telephonist
Grammar: gerunds
Vocabulary: words that go together
Grammar: *while/during*
Vocabulary: opposites
Grammar: prepositions
Writing: description of skills and abilities

Unit 14 (pp50–52)
Conversation management: job interview
Grammar: relative clauses
Vocabulary: words that go together
Sounds and spelling
Grammar: open and closed questions
Vocabulary: opposites
Writing: interview questions

Unit 15 (pp53–55)
Conversation management: typical beginnings
Grammar: reported speech
Vocabulary: meanings
Grammar: direct speech
Spelling
Vocabulary: negotiating
Grammar: negative questions
Writing: personal letter

Unit 16 (pp56–58)
Conversation management: useful expressions
Grammar: Present/Past/Past Perfect
Grammar: Past Perfect/Past Simple
Vocabulary: problem words
Grammar: verb patterns (A or B?)
Grammar: contractions
Vocabulary: noun or verb?
Writing: picture story

Test 4 (p59)
A Grammar
B Vocabulary
C Word formation
D Writing

Review

Grammar: question words

1

Fill in the gaps.

1 <u>What</u> is your name?
2 _____ were you born?
3 _____ old are you?
4 _____ kind of food do you like?
5 _____ are two things you don't like about living in London?
6 _____ don't you like them?

Kate Crawford.
In Melbourne.
Twenty-seven.
Italian and Japanese.
The winters and the 28 bus!
The winters are too long and the 28 bus is too slow.

Grammar: questions with *how*

2

Use these words to complete the questions:
long, often, well, soon, many, far, much.

1 How <u>many</u> people work for Tom MacDonald's company?
2 How _____ does Tom go to the cinema?
3 How _____ is the nearest cinema?
4 How _____ does Tom speak French?
5 How _____ does Tom's boss want the report?
6 How _____ does it take to fly to Canada from London?
7 How _____ does a good pair of shoes cost in your country?

Grammar: pronouns

3

Correct the mistake in the second sentence.

1 Tessa lives near Heathrow airport. ~~His~~ flat is in Wimbledon. <u>Her</u>
2 My sister studied medicine. He is a doctor. _____
3 I love Japanese food! Sashimi is your favourite dish. _____
4 Our flat is very large. Come and stay with them next time you visit Sydney. _____
5 Excuse me, is this your passport? I think you dropped him. _____
6 There are two rude men in Tessa's office. She doesn't like her. _____

Grammar: sentences with *going to*

4

Fill in the gaps in these sentences. Some will need more than one word.

1 Look at those clouds! I'm sure it's going to ___rain___ and I haven't got my umbrella.

2 The bus is late again. I'm _____ to start driving to work again.

3 I've got an important translation to finish and _____ to be late for work.

4 This is the second time this week. My boss _____ get angry soon.

5 _____ you going to call a taxi? Can I share it with you?

6 There's one! No. Those people _____ going to take it.

Grammar: adverbs of frequency

5

Correct the mistakes in these sentences and then write the sentences again with the adverbs in the normal position.

1 I go to the cinema alone never.
   I never go to the cinema alone.

2 Do you work usually on Saturdays?
   _____

3 Do you play tennis how often?
   _____

4 My boss has lunch always in a restaurant.
   _____

5 My flatmate and I go sometimes for a walk on Sunday afternoons.
   _____

6 I go to now and then a discotheque.
   _____

7 Does your boss travel ever to Malaysia?
   _____

Vocabulary: odd one out

6

Cross out the word that doesn't belong and add a word which does belong.

1 month, day, ~~Tuesday~~, week, ___year___

2 February, Saturday, Sunday, Monday, _____

3 evening, tomorrow, afternoon, night, _____

4 dinner, food, breakfast, supper, _____

5 knife, fork, sock, _____

6 stockings, spoon, tights, _____

Review

Spelling

7

Make adjectives from these jumbled letters.

1 pleantas p<u>leasant</u>
2 eforing   fo_____
3 shiglen   En_____
4 clasalsic cl_____
5 alictyp   ty_____
6 hisnaps   Sp_____
7 ginles   si_____
8 iiantal   It_____
9 riemard   ma_____
10 nerfhc   Fr_____

Vocabulary: words that go together

8

Each adjective in exercise 7 that does not start with a capital letter goes well with one of these groups of nouns. Write the adjective in the space.

1 <u>pleasant</u> weekend, evening, woman, man, weather
2 _____ languages, travel, food, customs
3 _____ music, architecture, theory
4 _____ room, woman, man
5 _____ Spanish food, British weather, Swiss chalet
6 _____ man, woman, couple

Conversation management

9

Kate Crawford is talking to Sofia Papas at a party. First read Sofia's parts of the conversation and fill in the gaps. Then read the dialogue below and put Sofia's parts in the right order.

a) What do __you__ do?
b) Four – English, Greek, French and Italian. How long _____ you going to stay in London?
c) Since I _____ ten. My whole family moved there.
d) How _____ languages do you speak?
e) I haven't _____ a job at the moment. What about you?
f) I __was__ born in Greece, but I live in Australia now.

KATE: Where are you from?
SOFIA: 1 __g__
KATE: Oh, really? How long have you been living there?
SOFIA: 2 _____
KATE: And what do you do? Do you study or work?
SOFIA: 3 _____
KATE: Oh. I'm Australian too, but I work in a bank here in London.
SOFIA: 4 _____
KATE: I translate documents into English.
SOFIA: 5 _____
KATE: Three – French, German and English. What about you?
SOFIA: 6 _____
KATE: I'm not sure.

Grammar: questions

10

Make questions from these words.

1 long how stay going to are you London in
   <u>How long are you going to stay in London?</u>

2 like what would do you here to
   _____

3 you are going France to
   _____

4 when do you have to back Australia to go
   _____

5 like you would visit Scotland to
   _____

6 what like do evenings you to in the do
   _____

Writing

11

Look at the job advertisement and the letter of application. Put the parts of the letter in the right order and the verbs in the right form. (Don't forget to complete the date!)

WANTED
TRAINEE SALES STAFF
for our new branch in Chorley.
Young people. Experience an advantage.
Two referees needed.

Write to: The Sales Director, Century Hi-Fi,
115 Bridge Road, Chorley.

The Sales Director   22 Maitland Court
Century Hi-Fi   Manchester
115 Bridge Road   22 August 19___ ___
Chorley

Dear Sir or Madam,

___ I (**a**) (**enclose**) _____ the names of two referees. Mr White (**b**) (**be**) _____ in France at the moment, but he will be back on Tuesday.

___ From November to March, I (**c**) (**work**) _____ in a furniture store in Melbourne, Australia. I (**d**) (**enjoy**) _____ the job very much.

___ I (**e**) (**look**) _____ forward to receiving your reply.

___ I (**f**) (**be**) _____ twenty-three years old. I (**g**) (**finish**) _____ a degree in Media Studies at Deakin University last November.

___ I am writing in response to your advertisement which I (**h**) (**see**) <u>saw</u> in yesterday's Evening Echo. I would like to apply for a trainee sales position.

Yours faithfully

Sofia Papas
Sofia Papas

1

Conversation management

1

An interviewer is asking some questions (1–7). Look at the answers. Then complete the interviewer's questions with *Who, What, Where, Why, What kind of, How long, Which*.

1. __Where__ are you working at the moment? — At Dunn's Department Store.
2. _____ have you been working there? — For two years.
3. _____ work do you do there? — I'm a salesman.
4. _____ department are you in? — Men's clothing.
5. _____ do you want to leave? — I'm not happy there.
6. _____'s the problem? — I don't like my boss. He's a very stupid man.
7. _____'s your boss, by the way? — Walter Bailey. Do you know him?

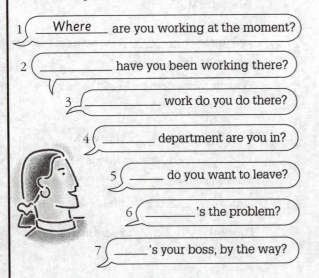

Grammar: questions

2

Make questions from these words.

1. your name what is
   What is your name?

2. you live where do
   _____

3. born were where you
   _____

4. you English learning have how long been
   _____

5. you English for your job need do
   _____

6. do you what do
   _____

7. doing you in your spare time like what do
   _____

Writing

3

This is what one student wrote in answer to the questions in exercise 2.

> My name is Klaus Bindseil. I live in Frankfurt, in Germany, but I was born in a small town called Peine. I have been learning English for five years now. I don't really need English for my present job but I think I can get a better job if I learn English well. I am a bank clerk but I would like to be a bank manager. In my spare time I like reading and playing tennis.

Now you answer the questions in exercise 2.

_____
_____
_____
_____
_____
_____

8

Vocabulary: opposites

One of the words in each second sentence is wrong. Cross the word out and write the correct word.

1 I can't buy that jacket. It is very ~~cheap~~.
   expensive

2 Things are very expensive in New York. The cost of living is very low. _____

3 I need some money. Can you borrow me some? _____

4 I'll earn more money in my new job. My salary will be worse than it is now. _____

5 In my job I have to speak French to my customers. That's why speaking is the least important skill for me. _____

6 I haven't heard from you for a long time. Did you send my last letter to you? _____

7 Things cost much more than they did last year. Prices are falling. _____

8 It is two o'clock in New York and seven in London. In other words it is five hours earlier in London. _____

Spelling

There is one error in each sentence. Cross it out and then correct it.

1 My husband ~~werks~~ in a bank.
   works

2 I can't see you now because I am very bisy. _____

3 Planes fligh very high in the sky. _____

4 What a wonderfull opportunity for you. _____

5 Give me a good reeson why you want to do this. _____

6 I hope we have enuf time to do this job. _____

7 My boss is yunger than I am. _____

8 I want to improove my spelling! _____

Sounds and spelling

Say these words aloud. Then match each word on the left with a word on the right which has the same vowel sound.

1 r<u>igh</u>t	f	a) f<u>oo</u>d
2 n<u>ee</u>d	—	b) h<u>ow</u>
3 w<u>or</u>d	—	c) r<u>ea</u>son
4 m<u>o</u>ve	—	d) g<u>oo</u>d
5 l<u>o</u>ve	—	e) <u>u</u>s
6 fr<u>ie</u>nd	—	f) f<u>i</u>ve
7 acc<u>ou</u>nt	—	g) g<u>ir</u>l
8 w<u>ou</u>ld	—	h) g<u>o</u>
9 kn<u>ow</u>	—	i) s<u>e</u>nd

1

Grammar: sentences with *need* and *should*

7

Rewrite these sentences using either *need* or *should*.

1 Is it necessary for you to use English in your job?
   Do you really ___need___ to use English in your job?

2 Is it a good idea for Tom to learn French?
   Do you think Tom _____ _____ French?

3 Is it a good idea for us to go now?
   Do you think we _____ ___ now?

4 Why is it necessary for us to do this?
   Why do we _____ to ___ _____ ?

5 How much time is necessary for you to do this?
   How _____ _____ do you _____ ___ ___ _____ ?

6 Is it a good idea for me to buy an English dictionary?
   Do you think I _____ ___ ___ _____ _____ ?

7 It isn't necessary for me to speak perfect English in my job.
   I don't _____ ___ _____ perfect _____ in my ___.

8 I think it's a good idea for us to do another kind of exercise now.
   I think we _____ ___ another _____ ___ _____ ___.

Vocabulary: words that go together

8

Cross out the noun that you can't use with the adjective in capital letters.

1 LONG   road   ~~woman~~   river   hair   flight
2 EXPENSIVE   clothes   prices   cars   meals
3 HIGH   prices   costs   rents   salary   money
4 LARGE   company   salary   profits   prices   losses
5 DIFFICULT   decisions   meetings   people   offices

9

Cross out the noun that you can't use with the verb in capital letters.

1 BORROW   some money   a dictionary   a car   ~~a message~~
2 RECEIVE   a letter   a phone call   a moment   some news
3 ACCEPT   an offer   the fact   a party   a gift
4 EARN   money   a reputation   a competition   a promotion

Grammar: *as, than, of, from*

10

Fill in the gaps in these questions (1–7) with *as*, *than*, *of* or *from*. Then match them with the answers (a–g).

1 Is Tessa older ___than___ James Chen?   ___d___

2 Have you been studying English for longer _____ the other students?   ___

3 What kind _____ books do you like?   ___

4 Where would you like to live ten years _____ now?   ___

5 Is the English word *economy* the same ___ the word in your language?   ___

6 Do you think English is _____ difficult _____ your language?   ___

7 Do you think monolingual dictionaries are better _____ bilingual dictionaries?   ___

a) No, but it's very similar.
b) Detective stories and books about ecology.
c) No. Japanese is very difficult for foreigners to learn.
d) I'm not sure, but I think she is.
e) No. We all started at the same time.
f) It depends on the dictionary.
g) Where I live now!

2

Conversation management

1

Choose the more polite alternative (a or b) for each part of the telephone conversation.

1 KATE: a) Could I speak to Tom MacDonald, please? *(circled)*
b) Get me Tom MacDonald. I want to speak to him.

2 RECEPTIONIST: a) Wait. He's speaking to someone else.
b) Could you hold the line for a moment?

. . .

3 RECEPTIONIST: a) He can't talk to you now. He's very busy.
b) I'm afraid he's not available at the moment.

4 KATE: a) Could I leave a message?
b) Take my message. Here it is.

5 KATE: a) Tell him to phone me back.
b) Could you ask him to call me back?

6 RECEPTIONIST: a) I can't hear you. Speak louder.
b) I'm sorry. Could you repeat that?

Vocabulary: words that go together

2

Which verbs can you use with each noun? Put ticks in the right boxes.

	money	(the) time	problems	dinner	a story
spend	✓				
tell					
have					

Grammar: Present Progressive

3

Which of these sentences refer to the future? Mark them 'F'.

1 Sofia Papas is phoning Kate Crawford. ___
2 She is spending next weekend in London and she wants to see Kate. _F_
3 She's having an interview for the job at Century Hi-Fi this afternoon. ___
4 Oh no! It's raining again. ___
5 Kate's going to a party on Saturday evening. ___
6 She's having dinner with some Greek friends tonight. ___
7 The Sales Director's interviewing more people for the new job this Friday. ___

Now make questions with the sentences you marked 'F'.

_2_ Where _is she spending next weekend?_
___ When _____
___ What _____
___ Who _____
___ When _____

Vocabulary: words that go together

4

Cross out the verb you cannot use with the noun in capital letters.

1 apply for get ~~reach~~ lose   A JOB
2 reserve book stay in buy   A HOTEL ROOM
3 cancel reserve make confirm   A RESERVATION
4 send receive fax attach   A FAX

Spelling

5

There are mistakes in each of these adjectives. Correct them and then write the words out correctly.

1 nece**s**ary   _necessary_
2 importent   _____
3 availible   _____
4 aceptable   _____
5 dificult   _____
6 pleasent   _____
7 confortable   _____
8 beautifull   _____

Vocabulary: opposites

6

What are the opposites of the adjectives in exercise 5? You can form six of them with the prefix _un-_.

1 _unnecessary_
2 _____
3 _____
4 _____
5 _____
6 _____
7 _____
8 _____

Grammar: questions

7

Make questions (1–5) and match them with the answers (a–e).

1. have study you do to evenings the in
   Do you have to study in the evenings? d

2. should I again it explain
   _____

3. post office the to would take letters these you
   _____
   _____

4. buy dictionary a bilingual I should
   _____
   _____

5. time tell the me you can
   _____

a) Yes. It's ten thirty.

b) I'm sorry. I can't. I'm waiting for an important phone call.

c) No. I think they understood.

d) No, but I usually look at some of the exercises again.

e) Yes, that's a good idea. Or you could get an English-English one.

Writing

8

Look at this fax message and choose one of the words in brackets to fill in the gaps.

FAX

To: Marc Braun
From: Terry Slater
Re: My visit to Barcelona
Date: 3 April
Pages: 3

This is to (1) *(promise/confirm)* __confirm__ that I will arrive on flight AF 310 at 10.00 on 14th May and leave on 16th May. Please (2) *(reserve/order)* _____ a single room with shower at the Oriente Hotel.
I am (3) *(attaching/putting)* _____ a copy of our current brochure. We haven't (4) *(had/received)* _____ the new brochure yet. Please (5) *(fax/write)* _____ any comments or suggestions (6) *(soon/immediately)* _____.

(7) *(Yours sincerely/Good health)* _____,

Terry Slater
Terry Slater

Now fill in the gaps in Marc's reply.

FAX

To: Terry Slater
From: Marc Braun
Re: Your visit to Barcelona
Date: 3 April
Pages: 1

We have just (1) __tried__ to reserve a room for you at the Oriente. They have no rooms available (2) _____ May 14th to 16th so I (3) _____ booked a room at the Via Hotel.
It is a bit cheaper (4) _____ the Oriente and is five minutes' walk (5) _____ our office.

We have not (6) _____ the last two pages of your fax today. Please fax these (7) _____ us before 8 p.m.

(8) _____

Marc Braun
Marc Braun

3

Conversation management

1

Put these expressions (a–g) in the best positions in the conversation below.

a) Just a moment.
b) What about a drink after work on the 14th?
c) Could we meet for lunch on the 12th?
d) I'll get back to you as soon as possible.
e) Let me check my diary.
f) Hello? Are you still there?
g) Hello, Kate. What a surprise! Where are you?

KATE: Hello, Terry? This is Kate Crawford.

TERRY: (**1**) Hello Kate. What a surprise! Where are you?

KATE: I'm in London, but I'm coming to Paris on the 10th.

TERRY: Great. When can we meet?

KATE: (**2**) _____

TERRY: That may not be convenient. I'll be in Lille that morning and I may not be back before the afternoon.

KATE: (**3**) _____

TERRY: Yes, that might be better. (**4**) _____

No, I'll be in Barcelona! Why don't you come for dinner on 11th? Margaret and the children would love to see you.

KATE: (**5**) _____
Someone's calling me on the other phone ...
(**6**) _____

TERRY: Yes, I'm still here.

KATE: I may have a meeting that evening but they'll confirm it next week. (**7**) _____

TERRY: That's fine. I'm looking forward to seeing you.

Grammar: would, could, Let's

2

Make these sentences more polite, using the word in brackets.

1 We will have dinner in a Chinese restaurant. (*Let's*)
   Let's have dinner in a Chinese restaurant.

2 Confirm that the Via Hotel is acceptable. (*Could*)

3 Bring the new brochure with you. (*Would*)

4 We will start the meeting an hour earlier. (*Could*)

5 Reply to this fax from Marc Braun. (*Would*)

6 You have to wait a few minutes. (*Let's*)

7 Get back to me when you know the date. (*Could*)

Grammar: may

3

Kate has made a list of things she wants to do in Paris, but she isn't sure she'll have time. Look at the list and write sentences with *may*.

> Paris trip
> Have dinner with Terry and Margaret on Tuesday
> Theatre on Monday if there's something good on
> Ring Marc Braun in Barcelona when I get to the hotel
> Visit the Louvre on Wednesday morning if it's open
> Buy some new clothes if I have enough money
> Meet Alan and Laura for a drink if they're available
> Stay in Paris for the weekend if I'm enjoying it

1 She <u>may have</u> dinner with Terry and Margaret <u>on Tuesday</u>.
2 There ____ not ____ anything _____ on at the theatre.
3 She _____ a friend in Barcelona when she _____ hotel.
4 The Louvre ____ not _____ Wednesday morning.
5 She _____ have _____ to buy any _____.
6 Alan and Laura _____ available.
7 She ____ stay ____ Paris ____ the weekend.

Vocabulary: words that go together

4

Which verbs can you use with each noun? Put ticks in the right boxes.

	a meeting	an appointment	a date
have	✓		
make			
be in			
hold			

Grammar: used to

5

Fill in the gaps in these sentences with *used to* and one of these verbs: *see, live, ski, speak, have, know, like*.

1 I <u>used to like</u> pop music, but I think today's music is terrible.
2 Kate _____ in Australia, but now she lives in London.
3 Tessa and Roger _____ each other every day when they were at Cambridge.
4 When Tom MacDonald lived in Canada, he _____ every weekend.
5 Sofia Papas _____ Greek more often than English.
6 People _____ more free time than they do today.
7 You _____ less English than you do now.

Sounds and spelling

6

Look at the underlined parts of each word. Match the words on the right with the words on the left with the same sound.

1 prom<u>i</u>se   <u>b</u>   a) inform<u>a</u>tion
2 c<u>ar</u>efully ___   b) k<u>i</u>ss
3 pl<u>a</u>nning ___   c) dis<u>c</u>uss
4 <u>arr</u>angements ___   d) in<u>cr</u>ease
5 <u>e</u>vening   ___   e) <u>y</u>ou
6 c<u>o</u>mpany   ___   f) th<u>ere</u>
7 <u>u</u>sed   ___   g) l<u>ow</u>
8 <u>o</u>pen   ___   h) perh<u>a</u>ps

Writing

Put the paragraphs in the right order. Then choose the right ending.

```
              The Director
              Snazzy Enterprises
              London WE2


              Dear Sir or Madam

         __ We look forward to hearing from you.

         __ The cost of the seminar, including all meals and
            accommodation, will be three hundred pounds.

         __ The seminar will take place at our centre in Oxfordshire.
            It will begin on Friday evening with cocktails and dinner
            and finish on Sunday after lunch.

         __ If you are interested in attending, you should contact
            Jackie Long by phone or fax on (0734) 345 654 or write to
            the above address.

         __ Next month we are offering a special seminar on 'Planning
            for the future'.

         _1_ Our company organises weekend seminars for people
            in business.

              Lots of love from/Yours faithfully/Goodbye

              Scott Emmerson

              Scott Emmerson
```

4

Conversation management

1

Read what A says (1–8). Find a good answer (a–h).

1. I've lost my job. _g_
2. You know that job I applied for? Well, I've just heard that I got it. __
3. The sales of our new product have been very low. __
4. We're very satisfied with the work you've done for us so far. __
5. Can you lend me some money? __
6. Do you mind if I use your phone? __
7. You're late again! And you were late twice last week, too. __
8. I got a very bad mark in the last test we did. __

a) Yes, I know. The figures are very disappointing.
b) Don't worry too much about it. Perhaps you'll do better next time.
c) Congratulations. That's wonderful news, isn't it?
d) Thank you very much.
e) I'm very sorry. It won't happen again.
f) Of course not. Go ahead.
g) I'm very sorry to hear that.
h) I'm afraid I haven't got any.

Grammar: verb forms

2

Complete the table.

Present Simple	Present Simple	Past Participle
go/goes	1 went	2
spend/3	4	spent
5 /has	6	7
rise/rises	8	9
fall/10	11	12
13 /14	15	done
leave/leaves	16	17
speak/18	19	20

17

Grammar: Present Perfect/Past Simple

3

Complete the sentences with the correct form of the verbs in brackets.

1 _Did_ your company's sales _rise_ last year? (*rise*)
2 _____ Roger _____ the figures carefully before he saw Dell? (*study*)
3 How many English words _____ you _____ so far this month? (*learn*)
4 _____ your teacher _____ you to learn any words yesterday? (*tell*)
5 The best film I _____ last year was *Les Enfants du Paradis*. (*see*)
6 Sales _____ by 15 per cent so far this year. (*fall*)
7 What _____ you _____ at the weekend? (*do*)

Grammar: questions and answers

4

Complete the questions to match the answers.

1 A: Have _you had_ a good day?
  B: Yes, I did a lot of work this morning.
2 A: _____ had lunch?
  B: Yes, I went out for a sandwich at one o'clock.
3 A: _____ ever used a word processor?
  B: Yes, I used a word processor for the first time in 1989.
4 A: _____ you written any letters this week?
  B: Yes, I wrote three letters last night.
5 A: Have _____ any new words this week?
  B: Yes, we learnt 'market' and 'share' in class yesterday.
6 A: _____ you _____ any good films this week?
  B: Yes. I saw a really good film on Tuesday night.

Vocabulary: words that go together

5

Cross out the word or phrase that doesn't belong.

1 WATCH carefully a ~~newspaper article~~ TV
2 SEE carefully these reports the film at the Odeon
3 LOOK AT these figures carefully the football match Kate
4 NOTICE carefully the colour of Kate's dress the flight number on the ticket

Grammar: adjectives and adverbs

6

Complete the table.

Adjective	Adverb
1 careful	carefully
nervous	2
clear	3
4	calmly
angry	5
good	6
7	quickly
fluent	8

18

7

Circle the correct word in these sentences. Then write the correct sentences out in full.

1 The film at the Odeon looks *(interesting)/interestingly*.
   <u>The film at the Odeon looks interesting.</u>

2 This cake tastes *delicious/deliciously*. What's in it?

3 I can't hear you very *clear/clearly*.

4 Your voice sounds *strange/strangely*.

5 This perfume smells *nice/nicely*.

6 The sales figures look *bad/badly*.

7 Dell Bradford sounds *angry/angrily*.

8 Listen *careful/carefully*. I'll explain it again.

Writing

8

Fill in the gaps in this memorandum with the correct preposition. (Don't forget to complete the date!)

MEMORANDUM

To: Tom MacDonald
From: Gladys Patak
Re: report on new project
Date: 14 May 19__ __

Please look carefully (1) <u>at</u> the figures (2) ____ the new project. Prepare a report to present (3) ____ the board meeting next Wednesday (4) ____ 10 a.m. Please include costs (5) ____ the new project and graphs (6) ____ your report.

The meeting will be (7) ____ the board room (8) ____ the fourth floor of our London office.

I would like to have a copy of the report (9) ____ Monday morning (10) ____ the latest.

Thank you.

Gladys Patak

Test 1

Grammar
A Choose the correct alternative.

1 _How_ old are you?
   a) How   b) How much   c) How many

2 _____ she like classical music?
   a) Does   b) Do   c) Is

3 That's my sister in the photo. _____ name is Laura.
   a) She   b) His   c) Her

4 I _____ born in Greece.
   a) am   b) was   c) were

5 Is your English better _____ it was last year?
   a) as   b) than   c) that

6 I _____ improve my typing. It's terrible!
   a) would like   b) need   c) should

7 She _____ a new course next year.
   a) is starting   b) starting   c) start

8 Let's _____ to the cinema tonight.
   a) going   b) go   c) to go

9 I used _____ to school every day when I was a child.
   a) walk   b) to walk   c) walked

10 _____ you noticed the colour of Tom's eyes?
   a) Have   b) Has   c) Did

Vocabulary
B Match the adjectives (1–5) with the definitions (a–g). There are more definitions than adjectives.

1 essential   _d_
2 acceptable   __
3 typical   __
4 single   __
5 calm   __

a) more or less all right
b) special or particularly useful or valuable
c) unmarried
d) completely necessary
e) quiet and not worried or excited
f) showing the main qualities of a group
g) extremely large

Spelling and word formation
C Form adverbs from these adjectives.

1 quiet   _quietly_
2 essential   _____
3 comfortable   _____
4 nervous   _____
5 careful   _____
6 angry   _____

Writing
D Fill in the gaps in this letter.

```
                                    22 Allenby Road
                                    London, NE5
The Personnel Manager
Fina Foods UK Ltd.                  5 April, 19___
19 Market Street
Slough

Dear Sir or Madam,

I am (1) writing to apply (2)_____ the
position as Accounts Clerk you (3)_____
in last Friday's Evening Times.
I am 22 years old and I (4)_____ recently
completed a course in accounting (5)____ college.  I
was (6)____ accounts clerk at Furst
and Larsen Ltd. Unfortunately the company went out
of business (7)_____ Friday, but the work
was interesting and I learned a lot.
I (8)_____ a curriculum vitae and the
names of two referees.
I am available (9)_____ interview (10)_____
Monday (11)____
Friday every week, but I would prefer to come
(12)____ the afternoon because I have driving
        lessons (13)____ the morning.
            I look forward (14)____
hearing (15)_____ you.

Yours faithfully,

Bernadette Clements
Bernadette Clements
```

20

5

Conversation management

1

Put sentences (a–k) in the right order to complete the telephone conversation.

a) Not too far, sir. Shall I call a taxi for you?
b) Just a moment.
c) I'm afraid it's my mistake.
d) Good evening, sir. Can I help you?
e) My name's Slater. I have a reservation.
f) Yes, it is, sir. But we have no record of a booking for a Mr T Slater, I'm afraid.
g) Is that spelt S-L-A-T-E-R, sir?
h) Just take a seat, sir. I'm sure the taxi won't be long.
i) Yes, that's right.
j) Are you sure they reserved a room for you at this hotel?
k) I'm sorry, sir, but we have no reservation under that name.

RECEPTIONIST: (1) _d Good evening, sir. Can I help you?_
GUEST: Good evening. (2) _____
RECEPTIONIST: (3) _____
GUEST: (4) _____ T Slater.
RECEPTIONIST: (5) _____
(6) _____
GUEST: I don't understand. My clients here in Barcelona made the reservation a month ago.
RECEPTIONIST: (7) _____
GUEST: Yes. This is the Hotel Oriente, isn't it?
RECEPTIONIST: (8) _____
GUEST: Let me check the fax they sent. (9) _____. The reservation is for the Via Hotel. Is it far from here?
RECEPTIONIST: (10) _____
GUEST: Yes. Thank you.
RECEPTIONIST: (11) _____

21

5

Grammar: verb tenses

2

Choose the best alternative to fill each gap.

1 We _made_ a reservation a week ago.
   a) make b) made c) have made
   d) are making

2 I _____ your letter on 16 April.
   a) received b) receive
   c) was receiving d) have received

3 _____ any good news lately?
   a) Did you hear b) Have you heard
   c) Do you hear d) Hear you

4 I _____ back in Amsterdam since Wednesday.
   a) was b) am c) have been d) being

5 I _____ Kate lately. Is she away on holiday?
   a) didn't see b) don't see c) see
   d) haven't seen

6 Terry _____ at the hotel.
   a) has just arrived b) just has arrived
   c) has arrived just d) just arriving

7 I _____ a new flat last week.
   a) am finding b) found
   c) have found d) find

8 _____ dinner with Terry and Margaret when you were in Paris?
   a) Did you have b) Are you having
   c) Do you have d) Had you

9 _____ any good films recently?
   a) Do you see b) Are you seeing
   c) Have you seen d) Did you see

10 Kate _____ in Paris for three days. She really enjoyed it.
   a) is b) went c) has been d) was

Work and leisure

3

Match the beginnings of the sentences (1–8) with the endings (a–j). (Be careful – there are more endings than beginnings.)

1 I like to spend   _i_
2 When was the last time you __
3 James Chen   __
4 Nathalie Artaud tries __
5 Do you ever   __
6 I don't have   __
7 Most people   __
8 We haven't   __

a) been to the cinema for weeks.
b) enjoy good food.
c) liked the film?
d) much time for exercise.
e) go swimming?
f) went to a dance?
g) getting up early.
h) to get some exercise every day.
i) a couple of hours a week walking.
j) enjoys reading.

Grammar: Present Perfect, Past Simple, used to do

4

Fill in the gaps with the correct form of the verbs in brackets.

Kate (**1**) (*spend*) _has not spent_ much time with Tom recently. She (**2**) (*speak*) _____ to him on the telephone once a day, but she doesn't have much time now. Tom still lives in London, but they (**3**) (*not see*) _____ each other for two or three weeks. Kate (**4**) (*be*) _____ very busy lately and she spends a lot of time with friends from work. She (**5**) (*not know*) _____ many people when she (**6**) (*start*) _____ working in London. She (**7**) (*think*) _____ about her friends in Australia all the time then, but now she has a lot of friends in London.

Vocabulary: words that go together

5

Cross out the noun that doesn't belong.

1 GO TO   work   a party   ~~home~~   a meeting
2 HAVE   a game of squash   an appointment   a party   business
3 DO   business   friends   a favour   some work
4 MAKE   a meeting   friends   an appointment   an impression

Grammar: verbs and nouns

6

Complete the table.

Verbs	Nouns
decide	1 decision
2	production
impress	3
reduce	4
5	discussion
6	interruption
confirm	7
pronounce	8
9	reservation
10	explanation

Writing

7

Write these dates as you would at the top of a formal letter.

1 3/3/93   3rd March 1993
2 16/12/94 _____
3 28/2/95   _____
4 31/5/94   _____
5 20/7/93   _____
6 11/4/95   _____

8

Now put these names and addresses in the right order.

(1) Chorley, Sales Director, 115 Bridge Road, Century Hi-Fi, Geoffrey Smythe

Geoffrey Smythe
Sales Director
Century Hi-Fi
115 Bridge Road
Chorley

(2) Paris 75009, Terry Slater, Poirel International Ltd, Marketing Manager, Rue de Gaulle 24

_____
_____
_____
_____
_____

(3) Marc Braun, 60009 Barcelona, Catalaco SA, Director General, Diagonal 105

_____
_____
_____
_____
_____

(4) Kenway Electronics, London W18, 18 Windham Avenue, Managing Director

_____
_____
_____
_____

6

Conversation management

1

Match Maria's problems (1–5) with Sofia's responses (a–e).

1 I'm really disappointed. I didn't get the job. _e_
2 I think I've eaten something bad. I don't feel very well. ___
3 He was very rude to me. I felt really angry. ___
4 I'm really miserable. I want to go back to Spain. ___
5 I think it's better not to work too far from home. It's too lonely. ___

a) I can imagine. He's a very unpleasant man.
b) I know how you feel. Why don't you phone your parents?
c) I see your point, but sometimes it's necessary.
d) Perhaps you should lie down.
e) I'm sorry to hear that.

Grammar: *I don't know ...* + question word

2

Complete the sentences.

1 I don't know where Baker Street is.
   _____ (where is Baker Street?)
2 I don't know _____
   _____ (what does 'disturb' mean?)
3 I'm not sure _____
   _____ (where did I put my keys?)
4 We're not sure exactly _____
   _____ (where are we going to stay?)
5 I don't remember _____
   _____ (who is Herr Kernholz?)
6 I don't know _____
   _____ (why is she angry?)
7 I'm not sure _____
   _____ (what is the English word for this?)
8 Can you tell me _____
   _____
   (how long does it take to get to Victoria Station?)

Vocabulary: sentences with *feel*

3
Fill in the gaps in these sentences.

1 <u>How do</u> you feel this morning?
2 Do you _____ a drink this evening?
3 How _____ James Chen _____ the job?
4 I should sit down. I don't _____.
5 Do you feel _____ learnt a lot of English?
6 ____ this chair. It's really soft.

Grammar: prepositions

4
Match the beginnings of the sentences (1–7) with the endings (a–g). Use the prepositions in the box to join them.

| on | with | at | under | like |

1 <u>d</u> I spend a lot <u>on clothes and cosmetics.</u>
2 ___ She's arriving _____
3 ___ Would you like to have dinner _____
4 ___ I'd like to make an appointment _____
5 ___ We have no reservation _____
6 ___ What have I done _____
7 ___ Do you feel _____

a) my car keys?
b) that new restaurant tonight?
c) that name, I'm afraid.
d) clothes and cosmetics.
e) Dr Patak, please.
f) a drink?
g) Wednesday.

Grammar: indirect questions

5
**Make indirect questions with *Do you know*....
Then match them with the answers (a–e).**

1 (Anne/get/another job) <u>Do you know if Anne got another job?</u> <u>c</u>

2 (Richard/stay/The Hotel Metropole)
_____
_____

3 (Tom MacDonald/work/London)
_____
_____

4 (Roger/have/problems/work/lately)
_____
_____

5 (Tessa/talk/James Chen/yesterday)
_____
_____

a) Yes, he works for an engineering company.
b) Yes, she did. She gave him some good advice.
c) Yes, she did. She's working for some architects in San Francisco.
d) Yes, he's had some problems with Dell Bradford.
e) No, he stayed at another hotel nearby.

6

Vocabulary: communicate, inform, notify, contact

6

Choose the correct form of one of the verbs above to fill in the gap in each sentence.

1 We are pleased to _____inform_____ you of our decision not to close the London office.
2 She can't speak much English but she can still _____ very well.
3 How can I _____ you if your phone isn't working?
4 Could you please _____ me of your decision as soon as the meeting is over?
5 The manager _____ us when our contracts needed renewing.
6 Could you please _____ all our overseas staff and ask them to call me?

Spelling

7

Correct the mistakes in these words and write them out again correctly.

1 comunication _____communication_____
2 interupt _____
3 sugestion _____
4 discusing _____
5 includding _____
6 impresion _____

Writing

8

Choose the correct form of the verb in brackets.

The Sales Manager European Trading Bank
Mendecutti Design Birmingham Square
Via Ischia 63 London W1
Milan 20143
Italy 24th May 19__ __

Dear Sir

Thank you for (**1**) (*send/sending*) __sending__ us your sales catalogue.

We would now like (**2**) (*to order/ordering*) _____ the following items: 10 desk lamps and 6 digital clocks.

Could you (**3**) (*confirm/confirming*) _____ that the prices in the catalogue are correct?
I (**4**) (*am noticing/notice*) _____ that the catalogue you sent is dated 1993.
Could you also tell us when (**5**) (*do you expect/you expect*) _____ to deliver the furniture?

I (**6**) (*look/looking*) _____ forward to hearing from you.

Yours faithfully
Kate Crawford

Now fill in the gaps in the reply to Kate's letter.

(1) _____   (2) _____

(3) _____

(4) _____

Thank you (**5**) _____ of 24th May. We are preparing your order for shipping.

The prices for this year are a little higher (**6**) _____ in last year's catalogue. I enclose a copy (**7**) _____ our price list.

Could you (**8**) _____ me immediately if the new prices are unacceptable.

I look (**9**) _____

(10) _____

7

Conversation management

1

A hotel receptionist is asking a guest some questions (a–g). Put the questions in the right positions in the conversation.

a) Did you enjoy your stay with us?
b) Was your room comfortable?
c) Why did you think the breakfast service was terrible?
d) What was that, madam?
e) How do you think we could improve our bathrooms?
f) Do you think I could ask you a few questions before you leave?
g) What do you think we should offer our guests for breakfast?

A: Excuse me, madam. (1) *(f) Do you think I could ask you a few questions before you leave?*

B: Well, yes, I suppose so.

A: Right. (2) _____

B: Yes, I did. Well, there was one thing I didn't like.

A: (3) _____

B: The breakfast service. It was terrible.

A: (4) _____

B: Well, it was very slow and there wasn't enough breakfast.

A: (5) _____

B: A wider variety of bread and cereals ... oh, and fresh orange juice.

A: (6) _____

B: Yes, except for the bathroom.

A: (7) _____

B: More space and hotter water!

Grammar: question word + *do you think...?*

2

Make questions with ... *do you think* ... and match them with the answers (a–e).

1 (Why is it a good product?) Why do you think it's a good product? **b**

2 (How can we increase sales?) _____

3 (When can you deliver the furniture?) _____

4 (What will the price of the new software be?) _____

5 (Where did my assistant put that file?) _____

a) Well, it's very user-friendly and it's very efficient too.
b) I think he took it to the meeting with him.
c) We're not sure yet, but it will be cheaper than our competitor's product.
d) Before next Tuesday.
e) Translating the manual into Spanish may help.

7

Vocabulary: expressions with *reason, cause, result, effect*

3
Fill in the gaps with an appropriate word.

1 I tried drinking hot milk before I went to bed. But it didn't _have_ any effect. I still couldn't sleep.

2 The effect ___ sales was dramatic. They increased by 20 per cent.

3 The technicians still do not know the cause ___ the problem.

4 What are your reasons ___ applying for this job?

5 The _____ why I was late was that the traffic was terrible.

6 As a result ___ the recession a lot of businesses have closed.

Grammar: first conditionals

4
Fill in the gaps in these sentences.

1 If _I go_ to Paris on business next month, I'll phone Terry. (*go*)

2 I _____ the report more quickly if you give me all the information. (*finish*)

3 I _____ back to you if we need to change the arrangements. (*get*)

4 _____ at the figures carefully, you'll see that we're losing our market share. (*you/look*)

5 _____ a conference going on, it will be difficult to find a room. (*there/be*)

6 People will listen to what you say _____ eye contact with them. (*you/make*)

7 _____ the manual into Greek and German, sales will improve. (*you/translate*)

Grammar: cause and effect

5
Make sentences using *so* to join the effects on the right with the causes on the left. (Be careful! There are more effects than causes.)

Causes

1 He was feeling very tense _so he decided to take a holiday._ (h)

2 I had a very bad cough _____

3 They drank too much champagne at the party _____

4 Transport costs were higher last year _____

5 He used to arrive late for work every morning _____

6 We made our manual more 'user-friendly' _____

7 The marketing director was not very good _____

Effects
a) I was smoking two packets of cigarettes every day.
b) He was working too hard.
c) I decided to stop smoking.
d) They were celebrating his new job.
e) Sales were poor.
f) More people could understand it.
g) He was not sleeping very well.
h) He decided to take a holiday.
i) Our customers found our manual difficult to understand.
j) They took a taxi home.
k) Prices rose.
l) I advertised for another assistant.
m) The pound was worth less than other currencies last year.

Vocabulary: *spend, waste, lose, give up*

6

Choose the correct form of one of the verbs above to fill in the gap in each sentence.

1 I _lost_ patience with learning shorthand. It was too difficult for me.
2 She _____ eating meat two years ago.
3 He _____ his copy of the textbook last week.
4 Did you _____ much money on that lovely new jacket?
5 How much do you _____ on food every week?
6 Don't _____ your time looking for a new dress. That one looks very nice.
7 She _____ her seat on the bus for an old man with a walking stick on the way home from work yesterday.
8 He _____ a lot of money on expensive meals in fancy restaurants. There are lots of cheap bars and cafés near his office.

Writing

7

Use the prompts to write a complete letter.

Poirel International

Flying Pigeon Agency
25 Kowloon Boulevard
Hong Kong

The Marketing Director
Poirel International
Rue de Gaulle 259
Paris 75005
France

23rd September 19__

Dear Mr Slater,

The Flying Pigeon Agency/specialise/registering imported educational materials/Education Authority. <u>The Flying Pigeon Agency specialises in registering imported educational materials with the Education Authority.</u>

We think/your product/suitable/registration.
_____
_____

We be grateful/you send/software/user manual/express post.
_____
_____

Not hesitate/contact us/above information/ unclear.
_____
_____

We look forward/hear from you.
_____

Yours sincerely,

Michael Chen
Michael Chen

8

Conversation management

1

Kate has had a meeting with a difficult colleague. She's telling her boss about it. Complete the conversation with the phrases (a–h).

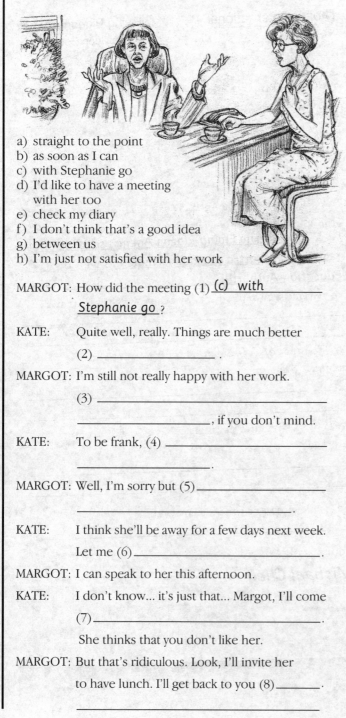

a) straight to the point
b) as soon as I can
c) with Stephanie go
d) I'd like to have a meeting with her too
e) check my diary
f) I don't think that's a good idea
g) between us
h) I'm just not satisfied with her work

MARGOT: How did the meeting (1) _(c) with Stephanie go_ ?

KATE: Quite well, really. Things are much better (2) _____ .

MARGOT: I'm still not really happy with her work. (3) _____ , if you don't mind.

KATE: To be frank, (4) _____ .

MARGOT: Well, I'm sorry but (5) _____ .

KATE: I think she'll be away for a few days next week. Let me (6) _____ .

MARGOT: I can speak to her this afternoon.

KATE: I don't know… it's just that… Margot, I'll come (7) _____ . She thinks that you don't like her.

MARGOT: But that's ridiculous. Look, I'll invite her to have lunch. I'll get back to you (8) _____ .

Grammar: passive

2

Make passive sentences from the prompts.

1 The French make very good perfumes. In fact, most perfumes/make/France
   In fact most perfumes are made
   in France.

2 The *Name of the Rose* was very popular a few years ago. It/write/Umberto Eco
   _____
   _____

3 The Japanese make cosmetics too. Some very good cosmetics/make/Japan
   _____
   _____

4 There was a terrible fire in a big hotel last night. A hundred and fifty people/kill
   _____
   _____

5 A: When/kill/John F. Kennedy?
   _____
   _____
   B: In 1963.

6 Tessa/offer/new job/a few weeks ago
   _____
   _____

7 A: When/this book/write?
   _____
   _____
   B: 1993.

8 A: Where/this book/publish?
   _____
   _____
   B: In England.

Key

Review Unit
1. 2 Where 3 How 4 What 5 What 6 Why
2. 2 often 3 far 4 well 5 soon 6 long 7 much
3. 2 ~~It~~ She 3 ~~your~~ my 4 ~~them~~ us 5 ~~him~~ it 6 ~~her~~ them
4. 2 going 3 I'm going 4 is going to 5 Are 6 are
5. 2 Do you usually work on Saturdays? 3 How often do you play tennis? 4 My boss always has lunch in a restaurant. 5 My flatmate and I sometimes go for a walk on Sunday afternoons. 6 Now and then I go to a discotheque./I go to a discotheque now and then. 7 Does your boss ever travel to Malaysia?
6. 2 February/Friday 3 tomorrow/morning 4 food/lunch 5 sock/spoon 6 spoon/socks
7. 2 foreign 3 English 4 classical 5 typical 6 Spanish 7 single 8 Italian 9 married 10 French
8. 2 foreign 3 classical 4 single 5 typical 6 married
9. b are c was d many e got 2 c 3 e 4 a 5 d 6 b
10. 2 What would you like to do here? 3 Are you going to France? 4 When do you have to go back to Australia? 5 Would you like to visit Scotland? 6 What do you like to do in the evenings?
11. 4, 3, 5, 2 a enclose b is c worked d enjoyed e look f am g finished

Unit 1
1. 2 How long 3 What kind of 4 Which 5 Why 6 What 7 Who
2. 2 Where do you live? 3 Where were you born? 4 How long have you been learning English? 5 Do you need English for your job? 6 What do you do? 7 What do you like doing in your spare time?
3. 2 ~~low~~ high 3 ~~borrow~~ lend 4 ~~worse~~ better 5 ~~least~~ most 6 ~~send~~ receive 7 ~~falling~~ rising 8 ~~earlier~~ later
4. 2 busy 3 fly 4 wonderful 5 reason 6 enough 7 younger 8 improve
5. 2 c 3 g 4 a 5 e 6 i 7 b 8 d 9 h
6. 2 should learn 3 should go 4 need/do this 5 much time/need to do this? 6 should buy an English dictionary 7 need to speak/English/job 8 should do/kind of exercise now
7. 2 prices 3 money 4 prices 5 offices
8. 2 a moment 3 a party 4 a competition
9. 2 than 3 of 4 from 5 as 6 as/as 7 than 2 e 3 b 4 g 5 a 6 c 7 f

Unit 2
1. 2 b 3 b 4 a 5 b 6 b
2.

	money	(the) time	problems	dinner	a story
spend	✓	✓			
tell		✓			✓
have		✓	✓	✓	

3. 3, 5, 6, 7 3 is she having the interview at Century Hi-Fi? 5 is Kate doing on Saturday evening? 6 is she having dinner with tonight? 7 is the Sales Director interviewing more people for the new job?
4. 2 buy 3 reserve 4 fax
5. 2 important 3 available 4 acceptable 5 difficult 6 pleasant 7 comfortable 8 beautiful
6. 2 unimportant 3 unavailable 4 unacceptable 5 easy 6 unpleasant 7 uncomfortable 8 ugly
7. 2 Should I explain it again? 3 Would you take these letters to the post office? 4 Should I buy a bilingual dictionary? 5 Can you tell me the time? 2 c 3 b 4 e 5 a
8. 2 reserve 3 attaching 4 received 5 fax 6 immediately 7 Yours sincerely
   Marc's reply: 2 from 3 have 4 than 5 from 6 received 7 to 8 Yours sincerely

Unit 3
1. 2 c 3 b 4 e 5 a 6 f 7 d
2. 2 Could you confirm that the Via Hotel is acceptable? 3 Would you bring the new brochure with you? 4 Could we start the meeting an hour earlier? 5 Would you reply to this fax from Marc Braun? 6 Let's wait a few minutes. 7 Could you get back to me when you know the date?
3. 2 may/be/good 3 may ring/gets to the 4 may/be open on 5 may not/enough money/new clothes 6 may not be 7 may/in/for
4.

	a meeting	an appointment	a date
have	✓	✓	✓
make		✓	✓
be in	✓		
hold	✓		

5. 2 used to live 3 used to see 4 used to ski 5 used to speak 6 used to have 7 used to know
6. 2 f 3 h 4 a 5 d 6 c 7 e 8 g
7. 6, 4, 3, 5, 2, 1 Yours faithfully

Unit 4
1. 2 c 3 a 4 d 5 h 6 f 7 e 8 b
2. 2 gone 3 spends 4 spent 5 have 6 had 7 had 8 rose 9 risen 10 falls 11 fell 12 fallen 13 do 14 does 15 did 16 left 17 left 18 speaks 19 spoke 20 spoken
3. 2 Did/study 3 have/learnt 4 Did/tell 5 saw 6 have fallen 7 did/do
4. 2 Have you 3 Have you 4 Have 5 you learnt 6 Have/seen
5. 2 carefully 3 the football match 4 carefully
6. 2 nervously 3 clearly 4 calm 5 angrily 6 well 7 quick 8 fluently
7. 2 This cake tastes delicious. 3 I can't hear you very clearly. 4 Your voice sounds strange. 5 This perfume smells nice. 6 The sales figures look bad. 7 Dell Bradford sounds angry. 8 Listen carefully. I'll explain it again.
8. 2 for 3 at 4 at 5 of 6 in 7 in 8 on 9 by 10 at

Unit 5
1 2 e 3 g 4 i 5 b 6 k 7 j 8 f 9 c 10 a 11 h
2 2 a 3 b 4 c 5 d 6 a 7 b 8 a 9 c 10 d
3 2 f 3 j 4 h 5 e 6 d 7 b 8 a
4 2 has spoken 3 haven't seen 4 has been 5 didn't know 6 started 7 thought
5 2 business 3 friends 4 a meeting
6 2 produce 3 impression 4 reduction 5 discuss 6 interrupt 7 confirmation 8 pronunciation 9 reserve 10 explain
7 2 16th December 1994 3 28th February 1995 4 31st May 1994 5 20th July 1993 6 11th April 1995
8 2 Terry Slater
Marketing Manager
Poirel International Ltd
Rue de Gaulle 24
Paris 75009

3 Marc Braun
Director General
Catalaco SA
Diagonal 105
60009 Barcelona

4 Managing Director
Kenway Electronics
18 Windham Avenue
London W18

Unit 6
1 2 d 3 a 4 b 5 c
2 2 what 'disturb' means. 3 where I put my keys. 4 where we are going to stay. 5 who Herr Kernholz is. 6 why she is angry. 7 what the English word for this is. 8 how long it takes to get to Victoria Station?
3 2 feel like 3 does/feel about 4 feel well 5 you have 6 Feel
4 2 g on 3 b at 4 e with 5 c under 6 a with 7 f like
5 2 if Richard stayed at the Hotel Metropole? 3 if Tom MacDonald works in London? 4 if Roger has had problems at work lately? 5 if Tessa talked to James Chen yesterday? 2 e 3 a 4 d 5 b
6 2 communicate 3 contact 4 notify/inform 5 informed/notified 6 contact
7 2 interrupt 3 suggestion 4 discussing 5 including 6 impression
8 2 to order 3 confirm 4 notice 5 you expect 6 look
1 Kate Crawford, European Trading Bank, Birmingham Square, London W1 2 Mendecutti Design, Via Ischia 63, Milan 20134, Italy 3 Date 4 Dear Ms Crawford 5 for your letter 6 than 7 of 8 inform/fax/phone 9 forward to hearing from you 10 Yours sincerely

Unit 7
1 2 a 3 d 4 c 5 g 6 b 7 e
2 2 How do you think we can increase sales? e 3 When do you think you can deliver the furniture? d 4 What do you think the price of the new software will be? c 5 Where do you think my assistant put that file? b
3 2 on 3 of 4 for 5 reason 6 of
4 2 will finish 3 will get 4 If you look 5 If there's 6 if you make 7 If you translate
5 2 c 3 j 4 k 5 l 6 f 7 e
6 2 gave up 3 lost 4 spend 5 spend 6 waste 7 gave up 8 wastes
7 2 We think your product is suitable for registration. 3 We would be grateful if you would send the software and the user manual by express post. 4 Please do not hesitate to contact us again if the above information is unclear. 5 We look forward to hearing from you.

Unit 8
1 2 g 3 d 4 f 5 h 6 e 7 a 8 b
2 2 It was written by Umberto Eco. 3 Some very good cosmetics are made in Japan. 4 A hundred and fifty people were killed. 5 When was John F. Kennedy killed? 6 Tessa was offered a new job a few weeks ago. 7 When was this book written? 8 Where was this book published?
3 2 open 3 easy 4 late 5 cheap 6 calm/relaxed 7 slow 8 right 9 fair 10 light 11 careless 12 better 13 same 14 sorry 15 low
4 2 turn 3 office 4 flight 5 pleasant 6 visited 7 nervous 8 suggestion 9 confirm 10 receive
5 2 i 3 g 4 j 5 b 6 a 7 c 8 e 9 h 10 f
6 2 When do you want the report? b 3 What time does your flight leave? e 4 Will you be at home on Saturday morning? d 5 Can I see you this afternoon? a
7 2 on/last 3 of 4 until 5 for 6 by 7 after 8 from

Unit 9
1 2 j 3 e 4 f 5 g 6 k 7 h 8 c 9 i 10 l 11 a 12 d
2 2 were living 3 were driving 4 were wearing 5 was reading/was typing.
3 2 was living/found 3 arrived/was talking 4 asking (asked)/knew 5 looked/noticed/was snowing 6 told/was feeling/wasn't listening (didn't listen) 7 didn't hear/was watching
4 2 pain 3 ache 4 hurt 5 damage 6 hurt 7 dull 8 heavy
5 2 g 3 i 4 h 5 f 6 c 7 j 8 e 9 b 10 a
6 2 myself 3 yourself 4 herself 5 each other 6 ourselves 7 each other 8 yourselves
7 1 neck 2 shoulder 3 arm 4 elbow 5 wrist 6 hand 7 finger 8 chest 9 back 10 stomach 11 hip 12 leg 13 knee 14 ankle 15 foot 16 toe

Unit 10
1 2 b 3 b 4 a 5 b
2 2 f 3 b 4 a 5 d 6 e
3 2 had Marc Braun's number. 3 the meeting was 4 he didn't think he had/would have/the new offices. 5 her he wanted/before the evening. 6 her he was going to London for a few days. 7 He told her he wanted to see a friend, Kate Crawford, there.
4 2 Marc Braun's number 3 is in Barcelona 4 you want me/Marc Braun? 5 flight are you coming 6 Kate and I know each other.
5 2 ask for 3 ask 4 ask for 5 ask 6 ask for 7 ask
6 2 suggest 3 confirm 4 advise 5 complete 6 repeat
7 2 would go 3 would buy 4 would borrow 5 saw 6 earned 7 would see
8 2 e 3 b, d, e, f 4 a, g 5 d, f
9 2, 1, 3, 5, 4

Unit 11
1 d 3 e 5 g 4 h 1
2 2 look that word up in a dictionary 3 call a taxi 4 I show you how 5 I type the letter to Mr Braun now? 6 Shall I tell Tom about Kate's contract? 7 Shall I repeat that? 8 Shall I open the door?
3 2 suppose 3 think 4 hope 5 suppose 6 hope 7 think
4 2 f 3 e 4 g 5 a 6 d 7 b 8 c
5 2 word processor 3 bandage 4 tray 5 water 6 bricks
6 2 terribly 3 extreme 4 well 5 extremely 6 clearly 7 strange 8 fast 9 awfully
7 2 skills 3 workers 4 well-paid 5 technical 6 administrative 7 dirty 8 interesting 9 clean
8 Letter A is better. 1 Letter B has no addresses and no date. It should begin Dear Sir/Madam. The writer does not say when and where he saw the advertisement or the title of the job. He has not enclosed an application form or mentioned referees. 2 The letter is too informal: All the best. I hope you give me the job, by the way.

Unit 12
1 2 a 3 b 4 a 5 a
2 2 What did he say in the letter? c 3 Who stole Kate's passport? b 4 What did she do about it? e 5 Who tried to help Kate? a 6 What did he do? d
3 2 impression 3 attractive 4 financial 5 success 6 national 7 stress 8 important 9 difference
4 2 attraction 3 responsible 4 important 5 stress 6 difference
5 2 instance 3 responsible 4 decision 5 accident 6 advertisement 7 passport 8 development 9 extremely 10 manual
6 2 been trying/since 3 been going out/for 4 been behaving/since 5 been sleeping/since 6 been waiting/for 7 been living/for
7 2 One hundred and seventy-five pounds 3 Sixty-four pounds ninety-nine 4 Three quarters 5 A/One thousand pounds 6 Two hundred and thirty-four dollars 7 Four hundred and eighty pounds

Unit 13
1 2 d 3 f 4 e 5 c 6 g 7 h 8 a
2 2 managing 3 studying 4 underlining 5 applying 6 listening 7 writing 8 lying 9 phoning 10 developing
3 2 meeting e 3 solving f 4 working c 5 managing b 6 selling a 7 learning d
4 2 very 3 personal 4 clean 5 dangerous 6 manager
5 2 while 3 while 4 during 5 while 6 during 7 while
6 2 lazy 3 unqualified 4 unreliable 5 polite 6 unsuitable 7 ungrateful 8 interesting 9 well-paid 10 unimpressive 11 safe 12 unnecessary 13 clean
7 2 honest 3 ungrateful 4 unnecessary 5 unreliable 6 unimpressive
8 2 in 3 in 4 for 5 into 6 from 7 with 8 of 9 with 10 at 11 for 12 with

Unit 14
1 2 What do you mean (by) 'changes'? 3 Can you tell me a little more about that? 4 You were in charge of personnel. Is that right? 5 Could/Can you tell me why you are applying for this post? 6 Is there anything you want to ask/Do you want to ask anything about the job or the company? 7 Where would you prefer to work?
2 2 Kate met 3 translator who/that/with her contract. 4 has written a letter 5 is a Canadian who/that likes Kate 6 Roger Mitchum is one of Tessa's friends who/that knows Kate too. 7 What is the name of the square that Kate's bank is in? 8 Sofia Papas is the/a woman who/that Kate met at a party. 9 Melbourne is the city that Kate and Sofia both come from. 10 San Francisco is a city that Kate would like to visit again.
2 Terry is the friend Kate met in Italy. 7 What is the name of the square Kate's bank is in? 8 Sofia Papas is the/a woman Kate met at a party. 9 Melbourne is the city Kate and Sofia both come from. 10 San Francisco is a city Kate would like to visit again.
3 2 connect 3 combine 4 connect 5 mix 6 join 7 combined 8 mix
4 2 g 3 d 4 e 5 f 6 a 7 i 8 c 9 b 10 h
5 2 What do you know about her? e 3 Has she applied for a transfer? d 4 When did she apply for it? b 5 Is she interested in visiting San Francisco? f 6 Does Tom know about this? a
6 2 top/bottom 3 combine/divide 4 waste/save 5 dull/sharp 6 lift/drop

Unit 15

1 2 d 3 a 4 e 5 c 6 f

2 2 would be at home 3 she was going to Crete 4 to send her the brochure. 5 asked (her/Kate) if she wanted 6 She told her she would really like her new boyfriend. 7 She wanted to know if Kate/she would have time to come over to Paris before the summer.

3 2 change/mind 3 accept 4 turn

4 2 post some letters 3 have lunch 4 is going to buy 5 When are you/is she going to buy it? 6 I'm not sure.

5 2 accept 3 promise 4 refuse 5 agree 6 schedule 7 negotiate

6 2 with 3 for 4 at 5 by 6 for

7 2 Isn't e 3 Couldn't a 4 Wouldn't b 5 Hasn't c 6 Couldn't d

8 2 I haven't made up my mind yet, but I think I'm going to accept her/the offer. 3 She said the salary would be about $500 lower, but she would ask the people in the San Francisco office about cheap accommodation. 4 I have to give her an answer before the end of the month. 5 What do you think? Do you think I should negotiate a higher salary? 6 Give my love to Margaret and the children.

Unit 16

1 2 g 3 h 4 c 5 d 6 a 7 b 8 k 9 f

2 2 do 3 is 4 was 5 has 6 had 7 does 8 did 9 were

3 2 offered/did not have 3 had not noticed/did not accept/sat down 4 remembered/had seen 5 waited/ran 6 got/had gone 7 explained/did not have/told/had brought 8 got/had phoned.

4 2 met 3 left 4 told 5 surprising 6 waste 7 meet

5 2 She suggested a good hotel in Paris to our clients. 3 The waiter brought us the bill/brought the bill to us after we had finished our meal. 4 He described his flat to her in the letter she received yesterday. 5 He also gave her some addresses in San Francisco/gave some addresses in San Francisco to her. 6 He explained the problem with Dell Bradford to her. 7 Margot offered Kate a new job/offered a new job to Kate a few days ago.

6 2 had 3 had 4 would 5 would 6 had 7 had 8 had

7 2 distribution 3 description 4 definition 5 competition 6 explanation 7 suggestion/discussion

8 … I had left them in my office./… I couldn't find them./… had locked the (main) doors./… I couldn't get out./… and ask him/her to come and unlock the doors./… (that there was) a light under my office door.

Test 1

A 2 a 3 c 4 b 5 b 6 c 7 a 8 b 9 b 10 a
B 2 a 3 f 4 c 5 e
C 2 essentially 3 comfortably 4 nervously 5 carefully 6 angrily
D 2 for 3 advertised 4 have 5 at 6 an 7 last/on 8 enclose 9 for 10 from 11 to 12 in 13 in 14 to 15 from

Test 2

A 2 c 3 c 4 c 5 a 6 b 7 b 8 c 9 a 10 a
B 2 production 3 impression 4 reduction 5 discussion 6 interruption 7 confirmation 8 pronunciation 9 reservation 10 explanation
C 3 d 5 a 6 e 7 c
D 8, 3, 2, 7, 6, 5, 4 b) in c) in d) to e) with f) on g) with h) to i) in j) for

Test 3

A 2 a 3 c 4 b 5 b 6 c 7 a 8 c 9 b 10 a
B 2 b 3 f 4 a 5 e
C 2 eventually 3 attractively 4 fashionably 5 extremely
D 2 She asked if you could phone her at the bank before 5.00. 3 We only received one page of your three-page fax message yesterday. 4 Could you send the other two pages immediately? 5 Kate told me yesterday it would be difficult to translate the documents before Thursday. 6 She has a lot of work this week. 7 I hope this will not be a problem.

Test 4

A 2 a 3 a 4 b 5 d 6 c 7 d 8 b 9 b 10 c
B 2 d 3 a 4 c 5 e
C 2 dishonest 3 unreliable 4 unemployed 5 misunderstand 6 disagree 7 badly-paid 8 hard-working 9 polite 10 weaknesses

Vocabulary: opposites

3

Complete the table of adjective opposites.

new		1	old
2		closed	
3		difficult	
early		4	
expensive		5	
6		nervous	
quick		7	
8		wrong	
9		unfair	
10		heavy	
careful		11	
12		worse	
13		different	
glad		14	
high		15	

Spelling

4

Correct the typing errors in these words and write them out again correctly.

1 qui**c**k   _quick_
2 tern   _____
3 offise   _____
4 flite   _____
5 plesant   _____
6 visitted   _____
7 nirvous   _____
8 sugestion   _____
9 conferm   _____
10 recieve   _____

Vocabulary: opposites

5

Match the verbs (1–10) with their opposites (a–k). Be careful! There are more verbs on the right.

1 earn   _k_   a) waste
2 fire   ___   b) cancel
3 refuse   ___   c) rise
4 reduce   ___   d) arrive
5 confirm   ___   e) lend
6 save   ___   f) find
7 fall   ___   g) accept
8 borrow   ___   h) receive
9 send   ___   i) hire
10 lose   ___   j) increase
                 k) pay

Grammar: questions and answers

6

Make questions with the words (1–5) and match them with the answers (a–e).

1 banks what do time open here
    What time do banks open here?   c

2 when report want you do the
    _____

3 time flight your does leave what
    _____

4 at home on Saturday morning be you will
    _____

5 I afternoon see you can this
    _____

a) Yes, I'll be in my office until 6 o'clock.
b) By Tuesday evening. I want to take it to the meeting on Wednesday morning.
c) At 9.30.
d) Yes, I'll be back by 11 o'clock.
e) At 9.00 but I have to check in before 8.00.

Grammar: prepositions

7

Use the prepositions *after*, *on*, *of*, *for*, *by*, *until* or *from* to fill in the gaps in this letter.

Kate Crawford
36 Canfield Drive
London, NW 3

1 May 19__ __

Dear Miss Crawford,

I regret to inform you that your application (**1**) __*for*__ a new contract with our London branch was refused when the Review Committee met (**2**) _____ Friday. Your section head did not provide sufficient proof (**3**) _____ the need to employ a third translator.

Your current contract is valid (**4**) _____ the end of this month. You may decide to apply (**5**) _____ a transfer to one of our other branches. You should inform us of your decision (**6**) _____ 31 May. No transfer applications will be accepted (**7**) _____ that date.

Transfer application forms are available (**8**) _____ the personnel office.

Yours sincerely,

R. K. Johnson
R. K. Johnson
Chief Personnel Officer

Writing

8

Complete this form with your own details.

TRANSFER APPLICATION

Surname: ....
First name(s): ....
Date of birth: .... Place of birth: ....
Nationality: .... Passport number: ....
Issued at: ....
Current position: ....
Educational qualifications: ....
Briefly say why you have applied for a transfer. ....
....
....
Signed: ....

Test 2

Grammar
A Choose the correct alternative.

1 I __reserved__ a room two weeks ago.
  a) reserved b) have reserved c) reserve

2 Let me sit down for a moment. I have _____ got home.
  a) yet b) already c) just

3 People _____ longer hours in the 1940s than they do today.
  a) have worked b) usually work
  c) used to work

4 I don't know what you _____.
  a) means b) do mean c) mean

5 Can you tell us _____ the train takes to get to Oxford?
  a) how long b) what time c) how far

6 Do you know _____ it costs to go to the cinema in London?
  a) where b) how much c) when

7 If you _____ less sugar, you will lose weight.
  a) will eat b) eat c) eats

8 What _____ if we don't get the contract?
  a) happen b) happened c) will happen

9 These shirts _____ in Portugal.
  a) were made b) made c) have made

10 _____ back before 11 o'clock on Saturday.
  a) We will be b) We are c) We

Spelling and pronounciation
B Mark the stressed syllable in these words.

1 decision   6 interruption
2 production   7 confirmation
3 impression   8 pronunciation
4 reduction   9 reservation
5 discussion   10 explanation

Vocabulary
C Match the verbs (1–7) with the definitions (a–e). Be careful! There are more verbs than definitions.

1 prove   __b__
2 find   ___
3 record ___
4 nod   ___
5 lose   ___
6 waste   ___
7 give up ___

a) to be without something because you cannot find it
b) to show that something is certainly real or true
c) to stop doing something
d) to write something down or put it on a computer so that it can be looked at later
e) to use something wrongly or use too much of something

Writing
D Put these paragraphs in the correct order. Then choose the best preposition and write it in the space.

☐ Yours faithfully,
  Tony Ellis
  Public Relations Officer

☐ Dear Sir/Madam,

☐ 20 May 19__

☐ We look forward a) __to__ (to/from) hearing from you b) _____ (in/on) the near future.

☐ Just fill c) _____ (in/on) the enclosed form and return it d) _____ (to/at) us e) _____ (with/for) a cheque for one hundred pounds, or phone Suzie f) _____ (in/on) 0340 505505, and the job you've always dreamed of could be yours.

☐ If you register g) _____ (with/for) us, we will send your CV h) _____ (to/at) a long list of potential employers.

☐ We are an employment agency that specialises i) _____ (in/on) finding positions j) _____ (for/from) top sales people.

[1] TOP JOB
  121 Ridley Rise
  Harlow
  Essex
  CM20 8QW

9

Conversation management

1

Who said what? Decide if it was the doctor or the patient who said the following (a–l). Write each question or answer in the correct order in the spaces below.

a) What were you doing before you started watching TV?
b) What seems to be the problem?
c) Yes, more or less. Sometimes it's a bit further to the left.
d) I was working in the garden.
e) When did it start?
f) I'm not sure. I think about a month ago, but it was just a dull ache then.
g) What kind of pain is it now?
h) Is the pain always in the same place?
i) Were you doing anything unusual when you first noticed it?
j) I've got a terrible pain in my back.
k) It's almost unbearable. It goes on and on.
l) No, I was just watching TV.

DOCTOR: (1) _(b) What seems to be the problem?_

PATIENT: (2) _____

DOCTOR: (3) _____

PATIENT: (4) _____

DOCTOR: (5) _____

PATIENT: (6) _____

DOCTOR: (7) _____

PATIENT: (8) _____

DOCTOR: (9) _____

PATIENT: (10) _____

DOCTOR: (11) _____

PATIENT: (12) _____

Grammar: Past Progressive

2

Fill in the gaps with the Past Progressive form of the verbs in brackets.

1 I __was looking__ (*look*) at our new brochure when the phone rang.

2 Tom and Hilary _____ (*live*) in Toronto when I met them.

3 We _____ (*drive*) to the airport when I remembered my passport.

4 You _____ (*wear*) a dark blue suit when you came for the interview.

5 She _____ (*read*) the report and he _____ (*type*) some letters when Kate arrived.

Grammar: Past Progressive and Past Simple

3

Complete these sentences, putting the verbs in brackets into either the Past Progressive or Past Simple.

1 (*work/met*) Kate __was working__ in London when __she met__ Tom MacDonald.
2 (*live/find*) He _____ in a flat with some other Canadians when he _____ a job with an engineering company.
3 (*arrive/talk*) When the letter from the Personnel Office _____, Kate _____ to Tom on the telephone.
4 (*ask/know*) He _____ if she _____ any good Mexican restaurants in London.
5 (*look/notice/snow*) When he _____ out of the window he _____ that it _____.
6 (*tell/feel/not listen*) When Kate _____ him about her contract he _____ hungry, cold and tired and he _____ properly.
7 (*not hear/watch*) 'Sorry, Kate. I _____ what you said. I _____ the snow falling. It's just like home.'

Vocabulary: *ache, pain, hurt, damage*

4

Complete each sentence with one of these words:

ache pain hurt damage dull heavy

1 I've got terrible stomach __ache__.
2 She felt a terrible _____ in her leg when she broke it.
3 When I get a head _____ I usually take a few aspirin.
4 That was a bad fall. Did you _____ yourself?
5 The fire did a great deal of _____ to the building.
6 My feet _____. I've been standing up all day.
7 At first I didn't really notice it. All I felt was a _____ ache in my arm.
8 The storm caused _____ damage all over the city. Windows were broken. Roofs were blown away. Thousands of trees were blown down.

Sounds and spelling

5

The underlined letters in the words in 1–10 have the same sound as those in the words in a–j. Match them.

1 a<u>ch</u>e   __d__   a) wh<u>ere</u>
2 p<u>ai</u>n   ___   b) <u>f</u>uture
3 m<u>ou</u>th ___   c) <u>o</u>ld
4 h<u>ur</u>t   ___   d) ta<u>k</u>e
5 dama<u>ge</u> ___   e) l<u>u</u>ckily
6 sh<u>ou</u>lder ___ f) <u>i</u>njury
7 noti<u>c</u>ed ___   g) th<u>ey</u>
8 d<u>u</u>ll   ___   h) w<u>or</u>d
9 l<u>au</u>ghed ___   i) <u>th</u>ousands
10 v<u>a</u>ries ___   j) proce<u>ss</u>or

Grammar: *each other/themselves*

6

Choose the best alternative and write it in the space.

1 Tom and Kate haven't seen <u>each other</u> (*themselves/each other*) very often lately.

2 I taught _____ (*myself/me*) to use a word processor.

3 You can hurt _____ (*you/yourself*) if you jump off of a moving bus.

4 When Kate practises French pronunciation she sometimes talks to _____ (*her/herself*) in front of the bathroom mirror.

5 Tom and his sister still write to _____ (*each other/themselves*) every month.

6 My flatmate and I usually cook a hot meal for _____ (*ourselves/us*) in the evening.

7 Two of my colleagues at work dislike _____ (*themselves/each other*) intensely.

8 There's some beer in the fridge. Help _____ (*you/yourselves*)!

Vocabulary: parts of the body

7

Use these words to label the drawing: *neck, shoulder, arm, elbow, wrist, hand, finger, chest, back, stomach, hip, leg, knee, ankle, foot, toe.*

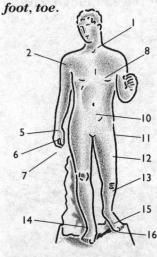
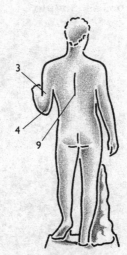

Writing

8

Look at Tom's diary.

> TUESDAY 5 JUNE
>
> Not a good day. Some new computers arrived for our department. I was helping Joe, the porter, to lift them onto the desks, when I felt a sharp pain in my back. I thought it would get better if I sat down for a while, but it just got worse. I went to the company doctor. He said it was lumbago. He gave me an injection and told me to go home and rest. The pain is still very intense.

Now write a paragraph about a time you hurt yourself.

10

Conversation management

1

Choose the most appropriate alternative for each part of this telephone conversation. (Note: Mandy is the telephonist.)

SOFIA: 1 a) Hello, my name's Sofia Papas. I'm phoning from Poirel International.
b) How do you do? I'm Sofia Papas from Poirel International.

2 a) Where's Marc Braun? I want to speak to him.
b) Could you put me through to Marc Braun?

MANDY: Marc Braun, thank you. I'm just putting you through. … Mr Braun.

3 a) Someone wants to speak to you. Here she is.
b) Sofia Papas from Poirel International on line 1.

MARC: Thank you. … Marc Braun.

SOFIA: 4 a) Hello, Mr Braun. Terry Slater asked me to phone to arrange the meeting next week.
b) Hi, Marc. You don't know me. I work with Terry. When's the meeting?

MARC: Oh, yes. We're all looking forward to Mr Slater's visit.

5 a) He must come here on Wednesday. The meeting is in the morning. If he is late, we will start without him.
b) What about the morning of Wednesday 18th? We could start the meeting at 10 and continue it over lunch if we need to, Oh, and we'd like him to see our new offices in the afternoon.

Vocabulary: *request* or *demand*?

2

Match sentences 1–6 with sentences a–f.

1 We requested a copy of your brochure.   c
2 She asked if she could have a refund.   ___
3 They asked for a table near the window. ___
4 She demanded a refund.   ___
5 We request that passengers carry only one piece of hand luggage.   ___
6 We asked where the manager's office was.   ___

a) I want my money back and I'm not leaving until I get it!

b) Could we have a table near the window?

c) We would like a copy of your brochure.

d) Please carry only one piece of hand luggage.

e) Could you tell us where the manager's office is?

f) Can I have my money back please?

Grammar: reported speech

3

These are some things that Terry said to Sofia yesterday. Put them into reported speech.

1 'How are you today, Sofia?'
   He asked her how she was.

2 'Do you have Marc Braun's number?'
   He asked her if she _____

3 'Is the meeting in Paris or in Barcelona?'
   He asked her if _____ in Paris or Barcelona.

4 'I don't think I'll have time to visit their new offices.'
   He told her _____ time to visit _____

5 'I want to be back in Paris before the evening.'
   He told _____ to be back in Paris _____

6 'I am going to London for a few days.'
   He told _____

7 'I want to see a friend, Kate Crawford, there.'
   _____

4

Look at Sofia's part of the conversation in reported speech and write what she actually said.

1 She said she was feeling a bit tired.
   'I'm feeling a bit tired.'

2 She said she had Marc Braun's number in her diary.
   'I've got _____ in my diary.'

3 She told him the meeting was in Barcelona.
   'The meeting _____.'

4 She asked if he wanted her to phone Marc Braun.
   'Do _____ to phone _____?'

5 She asked what flight he was coming back on.
   'What _____ back on?'

6 She said that she and Kate knew each other.
   _____

Vocabulary: words that go together

5

Complete these sentences with *ask* or *ask for*.

1 ask for information
2 _____ a refund
3 _____ a question
4 _____ an appointment
5 _____ someone a question
6 _____ another size
7 _____ why, where, who or when

Spelling

6

Make verbs from these jumbled letters.

1 cussdis   discuss   a problem
2 tesggus _____ a solution
3 firmonc _____ a reservation
4 viseda   _____ someone to do something
5 letepmoc _____ the sentences
6 eaterp   _____ the sentence after me

10

Grammar: second conditionals

7

Fill in the gaps. Use the correct form of these verbs: *buy, have, go, see, borrow, earn*.

1 If I _had_ more time, I would go swimming every morning.
2 Kate _____ swimming too if it weren't so cold in London in winter.
3 If Terry Slater were rich, he _____ a big house in the country.
4 If Tom didn't owe his sister three hundred pounds already, he _____ more money.
5 Most people would phone the police if they _____ someone stealing a car.
6 If Sofia Papas _____ more money, she would probably stop working and travel around Europe.
7 If Tessa accepted the job in New York, she _____ Roger Mitchum more often.

Vocabulary: *steal, rob, thief, burglar, pickpocket, shoplifter*

8

Match the beginnings (1–5) with the endings (a–g) to make sentences. (Be careful – more than one ending can go with most beginnings.)

1 The thief stole _b, c, d, e, f_
2 The pickpocket took _____
3 The burglar took _____
4 The gang robbed _____
5 The shoplifter took _____

a) the bank in the High Street.
b) our TV and hi-fi.
c) my car.
d) a leather jacket.
e) my wallet from my coat pocket.
f) jewellery worth £200.
g) three shops.

Writing

9

Put the sentences in the right order.

MEMORANDUM

To: Maria Pérez   Date: 8th June 19___
From: Marc Braun   Subject: Meeting

___ We would like to hold the meeting here in Barcelona.
_1_ Please contact Terry Slater and ask him to confirm our meeting on 18th June.
___ Tell him we need confirmation of the date of the meeting by 10th June.
___ Also ask him if he is going to bring their new software to the fair.
___ If that is not possible we could meet in Grenoble after the Expolingua fair.

Marc

Now write a similar memo from Kate to her assistant, Michael Johnson. She wants him to contact Terry Slater about the conference in Grenoble. She wants to know if Poirel are going to have a stand at the fair and if Terry knows any inexpensive hotels in Grenoble.

```
MEMORANDUM
To:            Date:
From:          Subject:
```

39

11

Conversation management

1

Which of the following (a–h) can you use when you want to offer to do something for someone else? Mark them O and match them with the responses (1–5) on the right.

a) Can I help you with those books? _O_ _2_

b) Could you explain how to do this exercise? ___ ___

c) Would you type these letters for me? ___ ___

d) Shall I close the window? ___ ___

e) Would you like us to book a hotel for you? ___ ___

f) Let's talk about it later. ___ ___

g) Do you want me to send it by fax? ___ ___

h) Shall I dictate the letter to you over the phone? ___ ___

1 Yes. Just read it to me.

2 Yes, thanks. They're awfully heavy.

3 Why? Are you cold?

4 No. I think we need to see the original.

5 No, thanks. I don't think I'll need to stay overnight.

Grammar: *Shall I...?*

2

Make these requests and demands into offers.

1 Help me with this bag!
   <u>Shall I help you with that bag</u>?

2 Could you look this word up in a dictionary for me? Shall I _____ for you?

3 Could you call a taxi for me? Shall I _____ for you?

4 Show me how to do it! Shall _____ to do it?

5 Can you type the letter to Mr Braun now?
   Shall _____

6 Tell Tom about Kate's contract. _____

7 Could you repeat that? _____

8 Open the door! _____

Vocabulary: *think, suppose, hope*

3

Fill in the gaps.

1. A: Do you think there will always be wars?
   B: I __hope__ not.
2. A: She's a very generous person, isn't she?
   B: Yes, I _____ so, but she's got a lot of money.
3. A: Is Kate going to stay in London?
   B: I don't _____ so. She has a problem with her contract.
4. A: They say the economic situation is improving. Do you think they're right?
   B: I _____ so, but I don't really understand economics.
5. A: Is English more difficult than other languages?
   B: I _____ not, but some things are difficult.
6. A: Is it going to rain?
   B: I _____ not. I haven't brought my umbrella.
7. A: Will you be here when I get back?
   B: I _____ so. I've got a lot of work to do.

Sounds and spelling

4

Match the words 1–8 with the words a–h that have the same sound in the underlined letters.

1. yo<u>u</u>ng — h
2. h<u>a</u>ppy — ___
3. j<u>o</u>b — ___
4. pl<u>ea</u>se — ___
5. tw<u>i</u>ce — ___
6. w<u>o</u>rk — ___
7. fr<u>ie</u>nd — ___
8. br<u>ai</u>n — ___

a) des<u>i</u>gn
b) v<u>e</u>ry
c) edu<u>ca</u>ted
d) f<u>i</u>rst
e) q<u>ua</u>lifications
f) gr<u>a</u>duate
g) p<u>eo</u>ple
h) c<u>o</u>mpany

Vocabulary: jobs

5

The words for people have been put with the wrong objects or materials. Correct them.

1. carpenter – ~~word processor~~ __wood__
2. secretary – water _____
3. nurse – tray _____
4. waiter – wood _____
5. plumber – bricks _____
6. construction worker – bandage _____

Grammar: adjectives and adverbs

6

Fill in the gaps in the sentences with the correct form of the word in brackets.

1. He speaks English very __fluently__ (*fluent*).
2. Close the window. It's _____ (*terrible*) cold in here.
3. It's a very pleasant climate. Even in summer we never have _____ (*extreme*) temperatures.
4. He always dresses very _____ (*good*).
5. I am _____ (*extreme*) grateful for your advice.
6. Could you speak a little more loudly? I can't hear you _____ (*clear*).
7. I feel a bit _____ (*strange*). I think I'll go and lie down for a moment.
8. She drives much too _____ (*fast*).
9. That's _____ (*awful*) kind of you.

11

Vocabulary: words that go together

7

Look at these advertisements for jobs and decide which of these words should go in the gaps: *clean, well-paid, technical, clerical, interesting, dirty, skills, administrative, workers*.

(1) __clerical__ Officer
To start immediately. Good pay and conditions. We want a responsible person who will be in charge of all our files and records. Word processing and computing (2) _____ an advantage. Application form from Jackie on 0734 546 388.

Construction (3) _____ Wanted
Looking for a (4) _____ job in the London area? We want carpenters and plumbers for building sites all over London.
Phone Max on 081 980 5412.

COMPUTER ENGINEER
Young and dynamic company in the Thames Valley needs someone with excellent (5) _____ qualifications to join our team of computer engineers. Some (6) _____ work involved.

Write to: The Personnel Officer, Linkatronics, Hamilton House, Bracknell.

Industrial Cleaners
Work cleaning used machinery. If you don't mind (7) _____ work for good money, phone Vince on 0273 998 345.

Work with flowers
We're looking for bright young people to deliver flowers in the Brighton area. (8) _____ work with lots of opportunities to meet people. (9) _____, smart appearance essential.

Writing

8

Look at these two letters of application for the Computer Engineer job advertised in exercise 7. Which one is better? Why?

```
The Personnel Officer            71 Wilcott Drive
Linkatronics                     Dorking
Hamilton House                   Surrey
Bracknell                        10 June 19___

Dear Sir/Madam

I am writing to apply for the Computer Engineer
position you advertised in The Echo of 9 June.

I have recently completed a degree in electronics. I
think I am suitable for the position you advertise.

I have some administrative experience as I have
worked for my uncle as a clerk during the months of
July and August for the last three years.

I enclose a completed application form and two
references.

Yours faithfully,
Myriam Clarkson
Myriam Clarkson
```

Dear Personnel Officer:

I am writing to apply for the job you advertised in the newspaper.

I've got a degree in electronics and some administrative experience.

I hope you give me the job because I think I'm better than all the other candidates.

Shall I send the application form too?

By the way, my name is Tim Saunders and I live at 42 Green Street, Brighton.

All the best,

Tim

Now do these tasks.

1. What is missing from the second letter? Add it!
2. Correct the inappropriate things in the second letter.
3. Write a letter applying for the job as clerical officer. Say where and when you saw the job advertisement; you have a diploma in computing; you had a similar job from May to September last year; you are enclosing the application form and the names and addresses of two referees.

12

Conversation management

1
Choose the best alternative (a or b) for the candidate's replies.

INTERVIEWER

CANDIDATE

1. Have you had any experience of administrative work?
   - a) No, I'm afraid I haven't.
   - b) Yes, I do. I am working in my uncle's office.

2. Do you think you would be good at working under pressure?
   - a) Yes, I think so. I always met the deadlines in my last job.
   - b) No, I don't think so. I like a relaxed atmosphere.

3. We'll make a decision about the job on Friday morning. Shall I phone you at home in the afternoon?
   - a) Yes, you shall. I will be there all day on Friday.
   - b) Yes. Have you got the number?

4. Could you tell me a little more about the course you did?
   - a) Yes. It was a course in marketing with Japanese.
   - b) Yes, I could. It was very interesting. I liked it very much.

5. Will you finish your studies this summer?
   - a) I hope so.
   - b) Yes, I will finish my studies this summer.

Grammar: questions with *who* and *what*

2

Make questions (1–6) and then match them with the best answers (a–f).

1 contract who Kate Crawford to wrote about her
   Who wrote to Kate Crawford about
   her contract? _f_

2 did letter what say in the he
   _____

3 passport stole who Kate's
   _____

4 did what do she it about
   _____

5 tried who Kate to help
   _____

6 did he what do
   _____

a) A policeman.
b) Someone on the underground.
c) He said she had to apply for a transfer by 31 May.
d) He told her to report it to the Australian Embassy.
e) She reported it to the police.
f) Someone called R K Johnson.

Vocabulary: adjectives and nouns

3

Complete the table.

Adjective	Noun
1 *responsible*	responsibility
impressed	2
3	attraction
4	finance
successful	5
6	nationality
stressful	7
8	importance
different	9

4

Now use some of the words from the table in exercise 3 to complete these sentences.

1 I was very __impressed__ by their new offices.
2 What is the _____ of working in London?
3 He has been _____ for all staff training at our head office.
4 Word processing skills are very _____ in most jobs these days.
5 Noise is a major cause of _____ in modern society.
6 What is the _____ between *skills* and *qualifications*?

Spelling

5

Correct the typing errors in these words and write them again correctly.

1 exemple (a) _example_
2 instence _____
3 responsable _____
4 decizion _____
5 acident _____
6 advertisment _____
7 pasport _____
8 developement _____
9 extremley _____
10 mannual _____

Grammar: Present Perfect Progressive with *for* and *since*

6

Complete these sentences.

1 Where have you been? I've _been waiting_ (*wait*) here _for_ an hour.
2 I've _____ (*try*) to phone you _____ three o'clock.
3 Tom and I met at a party. We've _____ (*go out*) together _____ about six months.
4 I know I've _____ (*behave*) a bit strangely _____ I heard about my contract.
5 I haven't _____ (*sleep*) very well _____ then.
6 It's very worrying. I've _____ (*wait*) for an answer from the Personnel Officer _____ nearly a month.
7 I've _____ (*live*) in London _____ three years now. It will be strange to work somewhere else.

Vocabulary: numbers

7

Write these numbers in words.

1 $207.50 _Two hundred and seven dollars fifty_
2 £175 _____
3 £64.99 _____
4 3/4 _____
5 £1,000 _____
6 $234 _____
7 £480 _____

Writing

8

Use the following notes to write a complete message.

> Claire phoned – 9.15 a.m.
> Can't come to work because hurt her leg at weekend.
> Has to stay at home and rest.

— MESSAGE —

Test 3

Grammar
A Choose the correct alternative.

1 I _____ a shower when the phone rang.
   (a) was having   b) am having   c) had

2 Do you mind _____ home early today?
   a) if I go   b) if I will go   c) if I went

3 My parents really loved _____. They always held hands when they went for a walk in the evenings.
   a) them   b) themselves   c) each other

4 Tom asked Kate _____.
   a) how she is   b) how she was   c) how was she

5 What would you do if you _____ someone steal something from a shop?
   a) see   b) saw   c) did see

6 _____ I help you with that suitcase? It looks very heavy.
   a) Do   b) Must   c) Shall

7 It was _____ of you to invite me.
   a) awfully kind   b) terrible kind
   c) extremely kindly

8 Who _____ the key to the computer room?
   a) did take   b) did he take   c) took

9 How long _____ English?
   a) do you learn   b) have you been learning
   c) are you learning

10 I've been using a word processor _____ 1988.
    a) since   b) from   c) for

Vocabulary
B Match the adjectives (1–5) with the definitions (a–f). There are more definitions than adjectives.

1 painful   d
2 dull   ___
3 connected ___
4 sudden   ___
5 satisfied ___

a) happening unexpectedly
b) not clear or sharp
c) unable to speak
d) causing pain
e) pleased or contented
f) related

Spelling and word formation
C Form adverbs from these adjectives.

1 awful   __awfully__
2 eventual   _____
3 attractive   _____
4 fashionable _____
5 extreme   _____

Writing
D Complete the phone and fax messages.

1 Kate Crawford/phone
2 She/ask/you could/phone her/the bank/before 5.00

Tom
1 Kate Crawford phoned.
2 _____
Gladys

3 we/only receive/one page/your three-page fax message/yesterday
4 could/send/other two pages immediately?
5 Kate/tell me yesterday/it be difficult/translate documents before Thursday
6 She have/a lot of work/this week
7 I hope this/not be a problem

```
          FAX MESSAGE
From:  Margot Barrios Whittaker
       European Trading Bank
To:    Ignacio Ramírez
       Galicom S.A
Date:  14 May 1993

Dear Ignacio,

3  _____
4  _____
5  _____
6  _____
7  _____

Regards,

Margot Barrios Whittaker
Margot Barrios Whittaker
Head of Documentation Services
```

13

Conversation management

1

Look at the sentences (a–h) below and put the conversation in order.

KATE: (1) <u>(b) Good morning. I'd like to speak to Terry Slater, please.</u>

TELEPHONIST: (2) _____

KATE: (3) _____

TELEPHONIST: (4) _____

KATE: (5) _____

TELEPHONIST: (6) _____

KATE: (7) _____

TELEPHONIST: (8) _____

a) I'll pass the message on to Mr Slater, Miss Crawford.
b) Good morning. I'd like to speak to Terry Slater, please.
c) No. I'm calling from London. Could you ask him to call me back? I think he has my number. I'll give it to you, anyway. It's 44 71 456 7234.
d) Who may I say is calling?
e) The line's busy at the moment. Will you hold?
f) My name's Kate Crawford.
g) I'll read that back to you: 44 71 456 7234. And I'm afraid I didn't catch your name.
h) Kate Crawford. That's C-R-A-W-F-O-R-D.

Grammar: gerunds

2

Complete the table.

Infinitive	Gerund
sell	1 selling
manage	2
study	3
underline	4
apply	5
listen	6
write	7
lie	8
phone	9
develop	10

3

Fill in the gaps in the questions (1–7) and match them with the answers (a–g).

1. Are you good at __working__ (*work*) in a team? __g__
2. Do you enjoy _____ (*meet*) people? ___
3. Do you think you are good at _____ (*solve*) people's problems? ___
4. Do you enjoy _____ (*work*) under pressure? ___
5. Are you good at _____ (*manage*) people? ___
6. Do you think you would be good at _____ (*sell*) our products to clients in other countries? ___
7. Do you enjoy _____ (*learn*) foreign languages? ___

a) I think so. I enjoy visiting other countries and I speak several languages.
b) Yes, I think I am. I had two administrative assistants working under me in my last job.
c) To be honest, I can't say I enjoy it, but I always finish the job!
d) Yes, I do. I've been studying Arabic in the evenings for six months.
e) Yes, very much.
f) I'm not sure. I'm good at solving my own problems and giving advice.
g) I think so. I prefer working with other people and I think people usually enjoy working with me.

Vocabulary: words that go together

4

Cross out the word that doesn't belong.

1. highly   well   ~~nicely~~   QUALIFIED
2. specially   highly   very   TRAINED
3. new   personal   important   CLIENT
4. stressful   dangerous   clean   JOB
5. dangerous   serious   personal   PROBLEMS
6. manager   administrative   executive   POST

Grammar: *while/during*

5

Complete these sentences with *while* or *during*.

1. __During__ the evening we talked about the new post.
2. Kate called _____ you were on the phone.
3. I'll call Kate _____ you write the fax.
4. Kate hasn't seen much of Tom _____ April.
5. She finds it difficult to keep in touch with friends _____ she's working.
6. She doesn't really like to go out in the evenings _____ the week.
7. Recently she even fell asleep _____ her colleagues were discussing an important translation with her.

Vocabulary: opposites

Find opposites for these adjectives. (Some of the opposites you can make with 'un'.)

1 honest __dishonest__
2 hard-working _____
3 qualified _____
4 reliable _____
5 rude _____
6 suitable _____
7 grateful _____
8 boring _____
9 badly-paid _____
10 impressive _____
11 dangerous _____
12 necessary _____
13 dirty _____

7

Now use some of your answers from exercise 6 to complete these sentences.

1 I am reading an extremely __interesting__ book at the moment.
2 Is it _____ to make personal phone calls from the office?
3 I don't want to seem _____, but I don't think I can accept your offer.
4 Staying overnight in Barcelona is an _____ expense. The meeting will be finished before three.
5 My memory is so _____ that I have to write everything in my diary.
6 The sales figures were _____ last year, but this year they are better.

Grammar: prepositions

8

Fill in the missing prepositions in this memo.

MEMO

From: Margot Barrios Whittaker
To: Chief Personnel Officer
Re: Transfer application
Date: 14 June 19__

Dear Mr Johnson,

I understand that you have asked (1) __for__ information regarding Kate Crawford.

Kate Crawford is (2) ____ charge of our Translation and Interpreting Services section here (3) ____ London. She is responsible (4) _____ all aspects of the service: the supervision of all translations (5) _____ English as well as translations (6) _____ English into the other European languages. She started working here three years ago when we advertised a post as translator for someone (7) _____ an excellent knowledge (8) ____ both German and French. She is an extremely reliable and hard-working person who can also be trusted (9) _____ confidential documents. We promoted her to section head late last year as we could see that she was good (10) ____ managing people and would enjoy the responsibility the post involved. Naturally we trained her (11) _____ the new position.

I believe it would be almost impossible to find anyone else (12) _____ Ms Crawford's skills and abilities. I would therefore recommend her for a transfer to any of our other main branches.

Writing

Write a paragraph about Sofia similar to paragraph two of the letter in exercise 8.

- in charge of accounting section
- responsible for all public relations and supervision of two assistants
- started here three months ago. Post advertised: Public Relations Officer
- well-qualified, hard-working, good at managing people
- excellent Greek, good French and Italian
- can be trusted with confidential information on clients

__Sofia Papas is in charge of our__
__accounting section.__
_____

Conversation management

Make the interviewer's questions from the prompts to go with the applicant's answers:

INTERVIEWER: Why/leave/last post? (1) _Why did you leave your last post?_

APPLICANT: There were some major changes in management structure.

INTERVIEWER: what/you/mean/'changes'? you/tell/me/little more/about that?
(2) _____
(3) _____

APPLICANT: Well, the company directors decided to bring in some management staff from their head office in New Zealand and one of these managers replaced me as Personnel Manager.

INTERVIEWER: you/in charge/personnel/that/right?
(4) _____

APPLICANT: Yes, that's right.

INTERVIEWER: you/tell/me/why/you/applying/this post? (5) _____

APPLICANT: Well, I'm qualified for the job, I have the right kind of experience and I'm interested in working for this company.

INTERVIEWER: you/want/ask/anything/about/job or company? (6) _____

APPLICANT: Yes. I notice you have a branch office in Bath. Would I be working there or here in London?

INTERVIEWER: where/you/would prefer/to work (7) _____

APPLICANT: In London. I've bought a flat here.

14

Grammar: relative clauses

2

Join the two sentences with *who* or *that* to make one sentence.

1 Sofia Papas is a woman. Terry works with her.
   <u>Sofia Papas is the woman who/that Terry works with.</u>

2 Terry is a friend. Kate met him in Italy.
   Terry is the friend who/that _____ in Italy.

3 Kate is a translator. She has problems with her contract.
   Kate is the _____ has problems
   _____

4 Margot Barrios has written a letter. It may help Kate.
   Margot Barrios _____
   that may help Kate.

5 Tom is a Canadian. He likes Kate very much.
   Tom _____ very much.

6 Roger is one of Tessa's friends. He knows Kate.
   _____

7 What is the name of the square? Kate's bank is in it.
   _____

8 Sofia Papas is a woman. Kate met her at a party.
   _____

9 Melbourne is a city. Kate and Sofia both come from it.
   _____

10 San Francisco is a city. Kate would like to visit it again.
   _____

In six of the sentences it is not absolutely necessary to use *who* or *that*. Write them out again without the relative pronoun.

1 <u>Sofia Papas is the woman Terry works with.</u>
   _____
   _____
   _____
   _____

Vocabulary: words that go together

3

Fill in the gaps in these sentences. Use *combine*, *connect*, *join* and *mix*.

1 <u>Join</u> the sentences by using *who* or *that*.

2 Can you hold for a moment? I'm trying to _____ you.

3 It's often difficult to _____ business and pleasure.

4 They're building a motorway that will _____ the two major cities.

5 To make mayonnaise, _____ the oil and the egg yolks slowly.

6 Would you like to _____ our group?

7 The socialists and the nationalists have _____ to form a government.

8 If you _____ the colours yellow and blue together, you make green.

Sounds and spelling

4

Match the words 1–10 with the words a–j that have the same sound in the underlined letters.

1 c<u>u</u>stomer — j
2 contr<u>o</u>l —
3 n<u>a</u>tional —
4 c<u>au</u>se —
5 w<u>oo</u>l —
6 resp<u>o</u>nsible —
7 r<u>a</u>nge —
8 t<u>ea</u>m —
9 l<u>i</u>ke —
10 se<u>r</u>vices —

a) q<u>ua</u>lified
b) cl<u>ie</u>nt
c) pr<u>e</u>vious
d) h<u>a</u>ppen
e) th<u>ou</u>ght
f) f<u>u</u>ll
g) b<u>o</u>th
h) n<u>ur</u>se
i) c<u>a</u>me
j) c<u>u</u>lture

Grammar: open and closed questions

5

Put the words in order to make questions 1–7 and match them with answers a–f.

1 anything you do know Kate about
   Do you know anything about Kate? __c__

2 about you do her what know
   _____

3 applied she has for transfer a
   _____

4 she when apply did it for
   _____

5 she San Francisco in interested is visiting
   _____

6 know Tom does this about
   _____

a) No, I don't think he does.

b) A couple of months ago. I think it was some time in May.

c) Yes, I know quite a lot about her.

d) Yes, she has.

e) I know that she's Australian and that she works for a bank.

f) Yes, she is. But she's been there before.

Vocabulary: opposites

6

Fill in each gap with two possible words from this list: *combine, waste, low, drop, high, top, divide, sharp, lift, dull, bottom, save*.

1 I'm looking for a flat near my office and rents are very __low/high__.

2 We walked slowly to the _____ of the hill.

3 The teachers decided to _____ the two groups.

4 Some people _____ money on clothes.

5 She told the doctor about the _____ pain in her left shoulder.

6 Be careful! That box is very heavy. Don't _____ it.

Writing

7

Look at this list of questions someone prepared for an interview for the job of Clerical Officer on p42.

```
Clerical Officer Post
1  Why did you leave your last post?
2  Why did you decide to apply for this job?
3  Are you good at supervising younger staff?
4  I see that you have experience with
   computers, but have you ever used a software
   package called 'Kontakwik'?
5  Do you enjoy working in a team?
```

Now write at least five questions for the 'Work with Flowers' advertisement (p42).

1 Why do you want to …
_____
_____
_____
_____

15

Conversation management

1

Match the beginnings in 1–6 with the endings a–f.

1 I've been thinking about it very carefully _b_
2 I can't make up my mind ___
3 I don't know how to tell you this but ___
4 I'm afraid ___
5 I'm glad to hear ___
6 I hope you won't ___

a) I don't really like the idea.
b) but I just can't make up my mind.
c) you've found another job.
d) about the job. Do you think I should take it?
e) that's completely out of the question.
f) change your mind about the new printer.

Grammar: reported speech

2

Look at the things that Sofia said to Kate on the telephone. Put them into reported speech. Use the verbs in brackets as reporting verbs.

1 I'm going to take swimming lessons. (*say*)
   She said she was going to take swimming lessons.

2 Will you be at home on Friday evening, Kate? (*ask*)
   She asked if Kate _____ on Friday evening.

3 I'm going to Crete in August. (*tell*)
   She told her _____ in August.

4 I'll send you the brochure. (*promise*)
   She promised _____

5 Do you want to come too? (*ask*).
   She _____ to come too.

6 You'll really like my new boyfriend. (*tell*)
   _____

7 Will you have time to come over to Paris before the summer? (*want to know*)
   _____

Vocabulary: meanings

3

Fill in the gaps.

1 When you '_make_ up your _mind_' you reach a decision.
2 If you decide to do something different you '_____ your ____'.
3 If you _____ an invitation you say 'yes'.
4 If you _____ down a proposal or a job you say 'no'.

Grammar: direct speech

4

Put these reported speech sentences into direct speech.

1 She asked if I was going to the post office.
   Are you going to the post office?

2 She wanted to know if I would post some letters for her.
   Will you _____ for me?

3 I told her I was going to have lunch in the office.
   I'm going to _____ in the office.

4 She told me the boss was going to buy a laser printer.
   The boss _____ a laser printer.

5 I asked her when she was going to buy it.
   _____

6 She said she wasn't sure.
   _____

Spelling

5

Look at these typing errors. Correct them and write the words correctly.

1 ofer   _offer_
2 acept   _____
3 promice   _____
4 rifuse   _____
5 aggree   _____
6 shedule   _____
7 negociate   _____

Vocabulary: negotiating

6

Complete the sentences with the missing prepositions.

1 What are the arguments _for_ and _against_ driving a car?
2 I don't often disagree _____ my colleagues.
3 They offered us £500 _____ our old computer.
4 We said it was worth _____ least £750.
5 They asked if we would bring the price down _____ £50.
6 They finally agreed to give us £700 _____ it.

Grammar: negative questions

7

Complete sentences 1–6 with verbs to make negative questions, then match them with the answers (a–f).

1. ___Didn't___ Ralph Johnson receive Margot's letter? _f_
2. _____ Kate worried about the transfer? ___
3. _____ she try to find a job with another bank? ___
4. _____ it be difficult to get a visa in the USA? ___
5. _____ Margot tried very hard to help her? ___
6. _____ she go back to Australia? ___

a) Well, yes, she could. Some other banks employ translators, but there aren't many jobs.
b) Yes. It probably would be difficult.
c) Oh yes, she's been very helpful.
d) Yes, she could, but she doesn't want to go back.
e) Yes, very. She can't take her mind off it.
f) Yes, he received it a week ago.

Writing

8

Read this conversation.

MARGOT: I've been talking to someone in our US office. He had an interesting idea. We thought you would enjoy working in our new office in San Francisco. I'm afraid it would mean a drop in salary, though.
KATE: How much lower would the salary be?
MARGOT: About $500 a month. But it's a very exciting post. I'll speak to San Francisco and see if we can arrange accommodation for you there.
KATE: It's a big decision. I'll have to think about it.
MARGOT: Yes, of course. You can't be expected to make up your mind just like that.

Now use the prompts to complete Kate's card to Terry.

1. Margot/offer/me/job/new San Francisco office/this morning!/I/very excited.
2. I/not/make up/mind yet, but I think/I/going to/accept offer.
3. She/say/salary/about $500 lower, but she/ask/people in San Francisco office/about/cheap accommodation.
4. I/have to/give/her/answer/before/end/month.
5. What/you/think? You/think/should/negotiate/higher salary?
6. Give/love/Margaret and/children.

Dear Terry,
Margot offered me a job in the new San Francisco office this morning.
I'm very excited.

16

Conversation management

1

Match the beginnings (1–9) with the endings (a–k). (Be careful – there are more endings than beginnings.)

1 I've heard you're looking __j__
2 She's got a strong background ___
3 I'd be grateful ___
4 Could you tell me ___
5 The factory closed and as ___
6 That's completely ___
7 I'm really looking forward ___
8 Let's not go on ___
9 She's made ___

a) out of the question.
b) to our next meeting.
c) a bit more about it?
d) a result I lost my job.
e) with confidential documents.
f) up her mind.
g) in electronics.
h) for your opinion.
i) sorry to tell you this.
j) for sales staff.
k) arguing about it.

Grammar: Present/Past/Past Perfect

2

Complete the sentences with one of these words: *was, were, is, does, do, did, has, had, are*.

1 What __are__ you doing tomorrow evening?
2 What _____ you want to do tomorrow evening?
3 Look out of the window and tell me if it ___ raining now.
4 When I looked out of the window this morning, it _____ raining.
5 Do you know how much rain _____ fallen in the last two hours?
6 When we got to the station, the train _____ left. We had to wait another hour for the next one.
7 Excuse me. What _____ this word here mean?
8 What _____ you do yesterday evening?
9 What _____ you doing at 8.35 yesterday evening?

Grammar: Past Perfect/Past Simple

3

Put the verbs in brackets into the right tense.

1 When the waiter __brought__ (*bring*) the bill I __realised__ (*realise*) I __had dropped__ (*drop*) my wallet somewhere.
2 My friend _____ (*offer*) to pay but she _____ (*not have*) any cash.
3 We _____ (*not notice*) that the restaurant _____ (*not accept*) credit cards when we _____ (*sit down*).
4 I _____ (*remember*) that on the way to the restaurant I _____ (*see*) a branch of my bank very nearby.
5 My friend _____ (*wait*) in the restaurant while I _____ (*run*) to the bank.
6 By the time I _____ (*get*) there, the manager and most of the staff _____ (*go*) home, but one of the windows was still open.
7 When I _____ (*explain*) to the cashier that I _____ (*not have*) my cheque book he _____ (*tell*) me that someone _____ (*bring*) my wallet to the front desk ten minutes earlier.
8 By the time I _____ (*get*) back to the restaurant the manager _____ (*phone*) the police.

Vocabulary: problem words

4

Choose the correct alternative and write it in the space.

1 Kate got to the bus stop a couple of minutes later than usual and she had already __missed__ (*missed/lost*) the bus.

2 Kate _____ (*knew/met*) Roger Mitchum at a party three years ago.

3 She stayed with friends that night because she had _____ (*left/forgotten*) the keys to her flat at the bank.

4 Someone _____ (*told/said*) me Kate Crawford was thinking of going to the USA.

5 That's _____ (*shocking/surprising*). I thought she was very happy in London.

6 She decided not to _____ (*lose/waste*) time looking for a job in Europe.

7 Roger says he can _____ (*look for/meet*) Kate at San Francisco airport.

Grammar: verb patterns (A or B?)

5

Use the prompts to write Past Simple sentences. Which sentences can be only pattern A (John gave Mary the book.)? Which ones can be only pattern B (John gave the book to Mary.)? Which can be both?

1 who/send/me/this book?
   Who sent me this book?/ Who sent this book to me?

2 she/suggest/our clients/a good hotel in Paris

3 the waiter/bring/us/the bill after we had finished our meal

4 he/describe/her/his flat in the letter she received yesterday

5 he also/give/her/some addresses in San Francisco

6 he/explain/her/the problem with Dell Bradford

7 Margot/offer/Kate/a new job a few days ago

Grammar: contractions

6

Does *'d* represent *had* or *would* in these sentences? Write *had* or *would* in the gaps.

1 I'd (would) prefer to stay in London.
2 I'd (_____) left my wallet in my other suit.
3 She'd (_____) met him a couple of times before.
4 She'd (_____) like to talk to you about the San Francisco job.
5 You'd (_____) enjoy living in New York.
6 He'd (_____) lived in worse conditions.
7 She'd (_____) liked him when she first met him.
8 He'd (_____) sent her flowers every day.

Vocabulary: noun or verb?

7

Fill in the gaps in these sentences with the noun form of the verb in brackets.

1 They gave us some very useful information (*inform*) about cheap accommodation.
2 They have had problems with the _____ (*distribute*) of their new software package.
3 She gave a detailed _____ (*describe*) of the company's new product.
4 Did you find a _____ (*define*) of 'software' in your dictionary?
5 There are so many cheap computers on the market that there is a lot of _____ (*compete*) between manufacturers.
6 He gave a very clear _____ (*explain*) of how the new system worked.
7 Can I make a _____ (*suggest*)? Why don't we stop for lunch and continue our _____ (*discuss*) this afternoon?

Writing

8

Look at these pictures and complete the story.

When I got to my car last night I realised I didn't have my car keys. I thought _____ _____. I went back to the office, but _____. I decided to get the bus home. I didn't realise it was nearly eight o'clock and while I was looking for my keys the security guard _____. When I went downstairs _____. I went back to my office to phone my boss _____ _____. Luckily the security guard noticed _____ _____. He let me out of the building and made sure I got to my car safely.

Test 4

Grammar
A Choose the correct alternative.

1 Is he good at _____ reports?
   a) to write   b) writing   c) writes   d) write

2 I am employed ___ a software company.
   a) by   b) for   c) as   d) like

3 He works ___ a clerk for a large company.
   a) as   b) like   c) by   d) from

4 You cut the bread _____ I cook the spaghetti.
   a) during   b) while   c) since   d) for

5 James is the young man _____ with Tessa.
   a) works   b) he works   c) what works
   d) that works

6 Why _____ to work with that company?
   a) you want   b) you do want   c) do you want
   d) want you

7 You said _____ be home by 11 p.m.
   a) you were going   b) you will   c) you had
   d) you would

8 What's the matter? _____ like the meal?
   a) Do   b) Don't you   c) You do   d) No

9 When I phoned the office he _____.
   a) left already   b) had already left
   c) already leaving   d) has already left

10 When I ___ there, she was already waiting.
   a) get   b) had got   c) got   d) was getting

Vocabulary
B Match the verbs (1–5) with the definitions (a–f). There are more definitions than verbs.

1 negotiate   _f_
2 trust   ___
3 motivate   ___
4 attract   ___
5 discuss   ___

a) provide someone with a reason for doing something
b) tell your secrets to someone
c) cause interest
d) to have faith in someone
e) talk about the details of something with someone else
f) try to come to an agreement through talking

Word formation
C Write the opposites of these words.

1 necessary   _unnecessary_
2 honest   _____
3 reliable   _____
4 employed   _____
5 understand   _____
6 agree   _____
7 well-paid   _____
8 lazy   _____
9 rude   _____
10 strengths   _____

Writing
D Tom MacDonald has applied for a job with another company. Look at the notes his boss has made and complete the letter of reference.

- has been with us for two years
- hard-working, trustworthy, good at working under pressure
- excellent skills and qualifications
- would recommend him

```
I am writing in reply to your
enquiry about Tom MacDonald.
_____
_____
_____
_____
_____

If you require further information,
please do not hesitate to contact
me again.

Michael Ellis
```

Longman Group UK Limited,
Longman House, Burnt Mill, Harlow,
Essex CM20 2JE, England
and Associated Companies throughout the world.

© Longman Group UK Limited 1994
All rights reserved; no part of this publication may be reproduced, stored in a retrieval system, or transmitted in any form or by any means, electronic, mechanical, photocopying, recording or otherwise, without the prior written permission of the Publishers.

First published 1994

Set in 10 on 11 pt Garamond ITC

Printed in Spain by Mateu Cromo.

ISBN 0 582 08543 8

Designed by Ken Vail Graphic Design

Illustrated by Kathy Baxendale, Sue Faulkes (Eikon Ltd), Angela Lumley (Specs Art) and Duncan Smith.

Acknowledgements

Dictionary definitions are based on the
Longman Active Study Dictionary.

We are grateful to the following for permission to reproduce copyright photographs:

The Telegraph Colour Library/Bill Miles for page 4 (left),
Tony Stone Images/Ken Fisher for page 4 (right).